By the same author:

Slayer: An Expanded and Updated Unofficial and Unauthorised Guide to Buffy the Vampire Slayer

Slayer: The Next Generation – An Unofficial and Unauthorised Guide to Season Six of Buffy the Vampire Slayer

Slayer: The Last Days of Sunnydale – An Unofficial and Unauthorised Guide to The Final Season of Buffy the Vampire Slayer

Hollywood Vampire: A Revised and Updated Unofficial and Unauthorised Guide to Angel (2 editions)

High Times: An Unofficial and Unauthorised Guide to Roswell

Inside Bartlet's White House: An Unofficial and Unauthorised Guide to The West Wing (2 editions)

SLAYER

A totally awesome collection of *Buffy* trivia

KEITH TOPPING

First published in Great Britain in 2004 by
Virgin Books Ltd
Thames Wharf Studios
Rainville Road
London
W6 9HA

ISBN 0 7535 0985 7

Typeset by Phoenix Photosetting, Chatham, Kent
Printed and bound in Great Britain by
Bookmarque Ltd

THIS BOOK IS DEDICATED TO

ANNA BLISS
AND
DIANA DOUGHERTY

The new man in Buffy's life is handsome teacher's assistant Riley Finn, but he, like her, has a secret identity – as a member of a military squad of demon-killers who implant a microchip into Spike's head that stops him from killing humans ('The Initiative'). Buffy and Riley discover each other's secrets when they come face to face fighting The Gentlemen, fairy-tale monsters who steal the voices of everyone in Sunnydale ('Hush'). The ramifications of this revelation cause complications for all concerned ('Doomed', 'The I in Team', 'Goodbye Iowa').

Willow meets shy lesbian witch Tara Maclay and the two begin a tentative relationship. Giles is briefly turned into a demon, the result of a spell by Ethan Rayne ('A New Man'). Faith wakes up from a coma, which she has been in since the Graduation Day massacre ('This Year's Girl'), and magically switches bodies with Buffy ('Who Are You?'), causing all sorts of mayhem and shenanigans before Willow and Tara reverse the effects. Neurotic, nerdish Jonathan Levinson performs an incantation that turns him into the most popular man in the world ('Superstar'). The only creature immune to the effects of this is Adam, the Frankenstein-like creation of The Initiative's now-dead leader, Maggie Walsh.

Yet another campus party gets supernaturally out of hand ('Where the Wild Things Are'), while both Oz ('New Moon Rising') and Angel ('The Yoko Factor') return to Sunnydale only to discover that their places in the affections of Willow and Buffy, respectively, have been superseded. As Spike, secretly working for Adam, sows the seeds of discontent and betrayal amongst the Scooby Gang, it seems that Buffy and her friends are drifting fatally apart. But they realise their folly in the nick of time and, together, summon the mythical power of the first Slayer to destroy Adam ('Primeval'), albeit with a few decidedly strange consequences, which manifest themselves in their dreams ('Restless').

The legendary vampire Dracula comes to Sunnydale to meet the Slayer about whom he has heard so much ('Buffy vs. Dracula'). But this is nothing compared to the surprises in store for the Scooby Gang when Buffy's sister, Dawn, is kidnapped by the incompetent vampiress Harmony Kendall and her gang ('Real Me'). Hang on ... Buffy's *sister*? Where did *she* come from?

Before that question can be properly answered, Xander's personality is accidentally split into two separate bodies ('The Replacement'), Riley suffers from the remnants of Initiative enhancement experiments previously carried out on him ('Out of my Mind') and Tara's terrible secret is revealed – that she's actually a perfectly normal human girl and not the demon that she'd always been led to believe she was ('Family').

However, the big news around Sunnydale is the arrival of bitchy, pan-dimensional goddess Glory, who is searching for The Key – a mythical energy weapon hidden by monks in the form of ... Dawn. Buffy is entrusted with this knowledge and told that she must protect the girl from Glory, who will use The Key to cause terrible destruction ('No Place Like Home'). Buffy pays Spike for information on his dealings with past Slayers and is given a harsh history lesson in the true nature of her calling ('Fool for Love'), while Joyce suffers from headaches ('Shadow') and is diagnosed as having a brain tumour ('Listening to Fear').

Buffy and Riley's relationship becomes unravelled due to misunderstanding and pride ('Into the Woods') and he leaves Sunnydale for a government-sponsored mission in South

America. Anya and Xander's relationship deepens when Olaf, a troll ex-boyfriend of Anya's, wreaks havoc in town ('Triangle'). The Council of Watchers arrive to check up on Giles, who is now running The Magic Box shop, but Buffy magnificently turns the tables on them and has Giles reinstated in his old job ('Checkpoint'). But she still has to contend with Spike's disturbing obsession with her ('Crush'), Dawn discovering her true status ('Blood Ties'), a love-starved android causing mayhem in the search for its creator ('I Was Made to Love You'), Joyce's untimely and unexpected death from a brain aneurysm ('The Body') and her subsequent funeral ('Forever').

As Spike forces crazed robotics genius Warren Meers to create a Buffy-replica sex toy for him to abuse to his heart's content ('Intervention'), Buffy and her friends try to stop both Glory and the crazed religious cult The Knights of Byzantium from learning the identity of The Key ('Spiral'). With Tara's mind having been painfully altered by Glory ('Tough Love'), Dawn is kidnapped by the goddess and Buffy becomes catatonic, Willow having to enter Buffy's psyche to pull her back from madness ('The Weight of the World'). Finally, Buffy realises that the only way she can stop Glory and save Dawn – and the world – is to sacrifice herself ('The Gift').

Determined not to let their friend remain trapped in what they believe to be a Hell dimension, Willow, Tara, Xander and Anya perform a resurrection spell that brings Buffy back to life. This occurs just as Sunnydale is invaded by biker-demons ('Bargaining'). What the Scooby Gang fail to realise – indeed, something that Buffy only confides to Spike – is that, rather than Hell, she was actually in paradise. She also confesses that she feels dislocated from the harsh and violent world that she's returned to ('After Life').

However, she is unable to dwell on such weighty theological matters as the trivialities of life, in the shape of various financial problems, threaten to overwhelm her ('Flooded'). She also has the attentions of a *Troika* of would-be super-villains, Warren, Jonathan and Andrew Wells, to cope with ('Life Serial'). Dawn's first date, inevitably, requires her sister to get her out of trouble ('All the Way') and, just when things seem as though they can't get any worse, a demon named Sweet casts a spell that forces the population of Sunnydale to reveal their innermost secrets through song and dance ('Once More, With Feeling').

Tara becomes disturbed by Willow's increasing dependence on magic as an answer to every problem and tries to force her to give it up. Willow's response – a spell to make Tara forget their argument – has disastrous consequences for the entire Scooby Gang ('Tabula Rasa'). The couple break up once Willow's foolish actions are revealed, though Willow is subsequently distracted from her pain when she finally manages to return Amy Madison, who has been trapped in the body of a rat for three years, to human form ('Smashed'). However, Amy's influence on Willow is not a benevolent one and she introduces Willow to Rack, a powerful warlock who eagerly feeds Willow's magic addiction ('Wrecked').

The *Troika*'s latest toy, an invisibility ray, gives Buffy the unexpected opportunity to, literally, disappear ('Gone'). Strapped for cash, Buffy takes a job at the local fast-food diner and discovers nefarious goings-on there ('Doublemeat Palace'). Meanwhile, Spike and Buffy find themselves trapped in a dysfunctional, abusive, no-questions-asked sexual relationship that neither quite understands. When the *Troika* kill Warren's ex-girlfriend, Katrina, they unsuccessfully attempt to pin the blame on Buffy ('Dead Things'), and the Slayer's birthday party is interrupted when a wish cast by Dawn is acted upon by one of Anya's vengeance-demon friends, Halfrek ('Older and Far Away'). Riley returns to Sunnydale with his new wife, in pursuit of an egg-laying demon ('As You Were'). Xander and Anya's wedding is ruined by the intervention of someone who claims to be Xander's future self but is, in reality, one of Anya's former victims ('Hell's Bells').

Injected by demon venom, Buffy suffers from powerful hallucinations, which suggest that her entire life for the past six years has been nothing more than an elaborate series of psychotic delusions ('Normal Again'). Having returned to the vengeance-demon fold after the humiliation of her wedding debacle, Anya tries to curse Xander for the pain that he caused her ('Entropy'). With Buffy finally realising that she's using Spike to ease her own pain, she tries to break up with him. Spike's response is an attempted rape of the Slayer. Buffy fights him off, then battles the *Troika* and captures Jonathan and Andrew, but Warren goes on the rampage and, in attempting to shoot Buffy, kills Tara instead ('Seeing Red').

A grief-stricken Willow tracks down and kills Warren ('Villains') before seeking vengeance on his friends ('Two To Go'). Stopped from carrying out her murderous plans by Buffy and Giles, Willow attempts to destroy the world in order to end her own suffering. She is prevented from doing so by Xander, who demonstrates his love for her ('Grave'). Meanwhile, overwhelmed with the guilt of his abuse of Buffy, Spike flees to Africa and, after undergoing a series of outrageously difficult trials by combat, he is rewarded with the return of his soul.

While Willow gains help for her addiction in England with Giles and a Wicca coven, a young woman is pursued through

11

the streets of Istanbul by robed figures and ritually knifed to death – the first in a series of similar incidents around the world. Someone is clearly targeting young women who share a similar potential and, while Buffy realises that this is happening through her dreams of these events, she can do nothing. Meanwhile, in Sunnydale, Dawn attends her first day at the newly reopened Sunnydale High, accompanied by her (frankly nervous) sister and they encounter a group of dead spirits in the basement ('Lessons'). A giant wormlike Sluggoth demon is on the loose in Sunnydale, the result of Anya's latest piece of deranged wish-granting. Xander and Buffy try to help the demon's intended victim, Nancy. Meanwhile, Spike tells Buffy about his re-ensoulment ('Beneath You'). Willow's return to America is hampered by her invisibility from her friends – a manifestation of her own secret fears – and by the presence of Gnarl, a flesh-eating demon ('Same Time, Same Place').

Buffy is offered a job as counsellor to troubled teens by the school's new principal, Robin Wood. One of Buffy's first cases is that of psychic girl Cassie Newton, who tells Buffy that she will soon die, a prediction that Buffy, despite her best efforts, is powerless to prevent ('Help'). Anya grants another wish, to a scorned college girl, which has devastating consequences. Horrified by the carnage that Anya has, inadvertently, caused, Buffy is faced with the awful decision to kill her ex-friend. However, Xander bravely standing up for his former lover and D'Hoffryn's sinister games combine to save Anya and give her a second dose of humanity ('Selfless'). Dawn's first major crush – on the school's star quarterback, RJ Brooks – surprises Buffy until she, too, falls head over heels for his boyish charms. And she isn't the only one. With all their female friends desperately battling to win RJ's affections by any means necessary, Spike and Xander team up to discover why the teen has such an infatuating effect on women ('Him').

While patrolling, Buffy meets a former classmate, Holden, who is now a vampire. Holden gets Buffy to reveal some of her insecurities but, shockingly, tells her that he was recently sired by Spike. Meanwhile, Dawn faces a night of horror as an invisible force trashes the Summers' home and she sees visions of her dead mother. And the ghost of Cassie Newton visits Willow saying that she's been sent by Tara ('Conversations With Dead People'). Most of these events are, subsequently, shown to be the work of The First Evil, the shape-changing non-corporeal entity who has been using Spike as an assassin, triggering a killing spree via an old folk song ('Sleeper').

The First's complicated masterplan has various strands, including appearing to the fugitive Andrew Wells in the form of Warren and getting Andrew to kill Jonathan and use his blood to open the Seal of Danzalthar, which caps the Hellmouth. The latter part of the plan fails, however, and Andrew is apprehended by Willow and held captive by the Scooby Gang. Subsequently, The First's minions, the Bringers, kidnap Spike and The First tortures the vampire, physically and mentally ('Never Leave Me'). Giles returns to Sunnydale with three potential Slayers – Kennedy, Molly and Amanda. He believes that The First's plan is to kill off the entire future Slayer line before opening the Hellmouth and unleashing the forces beneath. Buffy faces one such opponent, an ancient vampire, the Turok-Han. She is unable to defeat it ('Bring On the Night'). More potential Slayers arrive in Sunnydale. One, Eve, creates tensions within the group by claiming that Buffy isn't strong enough to protect them. Buffy and Xander subsequently discover Eve's body in a motel, meaning that The First has been amongst them for two days, sowing discord ('Showtime').

Having rescued Spike, Buffy and he commence the training of the potential Slayers. Willow attempts a locator spell and discovers that another potential Slayer is resident in Sunnydale. Remarkably, it seems that Dawn has been chosen as one of her sister's possible successors. However, everything is not as it seems ('Potential'). After sharing a kiss with Kennedy, Willow is magically transformed into Warren and must confront both the loss of Tara and the rage within her that turned her into a murderer. Meanwhile, Spike's chip begins to malfunction and Buffy asks The Initiative for help ('The Killer In Me').

Buffy goes on a date with Robin Wood in an attempt to discover if he has any hidden secrets. After they are attacked by vampires, he reveals that he is the son of a former Slayer, Nikki. Xander, too, finds himself a date on the same night. However, the gorgeous Lissa's interest in *him* is much more pragmatically demonic ('First Date'). Wood gives Buffy various items that belonged to his mother, including a sealed box. On opening the box, Buffy discovers a portal to the distant past. There, Buffy meets the originators of the Slayer line, the Shadow Men, who offer her power to fight The First, but at a huge personal price ('Get It Done').

Andrew attempts to film a video-diary-style documentary describing the current situation in Sunnydale for future generations. Meanwhile, the Seal of Danzalthar causes an outbreak of manic violence at Sunnydale High. Buffy and Willow force Andrew to recall the circumstances that led to Jonathan's murder in an effort to close the seal and stop the madness ('Storyteller'). Giles acquires a device that, he hopes, will deactivate The First's ability to trigger Spike into acts against his will. When used, it causes Spike to remember the close relationship that he shared with his mother when he was still human; after he was sired, Spike attempted to save his dying mother by turning her into a vampire, but the demon within her rejected Spike's plans for them to spend an eternity together and he was forced to kill her again – this time permanently. Meanwhile, with Buffy refusing to believe that Spike is a danger, Robin Wood asks Giles to help him gain his revenge upon the vampire who murdered his mother ('Lies My Parents Told Me').

Summoned from Los Angeles by Willow, Faith's arrival in Sunnydale brings tension to the Scooby Gang. There's another newcomer in town – Caleb, a violent Bible-thumping acolyte of The First with super-strength and a vicious line in misogyny ('Dirty Girls'). Following Caleb's blinding Xander in one eye, a guilty Buffy seeks revenge and a furious argument with Faith ensues about tactics and strategy. This culminates in the potentials choosing between their two leaders. Because of Buffy's recent rash decisions, the outcome is never in question. Meanwhile, Spike and Andrew investigate an abandoned mission and discover an important clue as to The First's weakness ('Empty Places, Touched').

Buffy finds the weapon that The First has been attempting to hide from her: a mythical axe embedded in stone. Faith and the potential Slayers are caught in the explosion from Caleb's bomb. With Buffy's help, they escape, return to Revello Drive and regroup for the final battle with the forces of darkness ('End of Days'). Angel arrives to help Buffy but their reunion is rudely interrupted by Caleb, whom Buffy kills. Angel gives Buffy an amulet to help her in the coming apocalypse. The First tells Buffy that the Slayer will always fight alone and, upon hearing this, Buffy has Willow create a spell that takes power from the Guardian's weapon and shares it equally among every potential Slayer. Buffy, Faith and their newly acquired army of young Slayers open the Seal of Danzalthar and battle the hordes of Hell. This leaves many dead, including Anya. Spike allows the amulet to consume him and the energy released from this devastates the Turok-Han masses. Spike and Buffy share a final moment together before Spike is, seemingly, destroyed. Buffy runs after the speeding school bus that carries her friends and they make it out of town just as Sunnydale disappears into a massive crater. As they look back to where the town used to be, Buffy and her friends speculate on what the future holds ('Chosen').

AWESOME!!!:
The best 30 episodes of *Buffy the Vampire Slayer*

Here is that imaginary desert-island six-DVD box-set of *Buffy* episodes that are, quite simply, impossible to live without. Just imagine how empty and worthless your lives would be if you'd been born in the eighteenth century and, as a consequence, never got to see the following:

'Hush' (episode 66)
Fairy-tale heart-removing demons, The Gentlemen, come to Sunnydale and steal everyone's voices.

'Once More, With Feeling' (episode 107)
Sweet, Hell's grooviest cat, forces Sunnydale's population to reveal their innermost feelings through song and dance.

'The Body' (episode 94)
The immediate aftermath of the wholly unexpected death of Joyce Summers brings all too human, everyday horror to the lives of the Scooby Gang.

'Doppelgängland' (episode 50)
Attempting to help Anya recover her lost amulet, Willow summons a pan-dimensional lesbian-vampire version of herself.

'Lover's Walk' (episode 42)
A lovelorn Spike kidnaps Xander and Willow in an attempt to

acquire a love potion with which to win back his departed Drusilla ... with hilarious consequences.

'Band Candy' (episode 40)
Ethan Rayne creates demonic chocolate bars, which, when eaten, revert Sunnydale's adults (mentally) to their teenage years.

'Fool for Love' (episode 85)
Spike gives Buffy a valuable history lesson in what it is to be – and to kill – a vampire Slayer.

'Bewitched, Bothered and Bewildered' (episode 28)
A bitter Xander asks Amy Madison for a spell that will cause Cordelia to fall madly in love with him, following the couple's break-up on Valentine's Day. Inevitably, it goes disastrously wrong.

'Chosen' (episode 144)
The First Evil's apocalyptic final plans are thwarted, through heroism and self-sacrifice, by the Slayer and her friends.

'Selfless' (episode 127)
Anya grants a wish to a scorned girl, which causes mayhem and bloody carnage and gives her the opportunity to reflect upon her past mistakes.

'Lie To Me' (episode 19)
Buffy's ex-boyfriend, Billy Fordham, arrives at Sunnydale High harbouring a dark secret and searching for a gift that will offer him a new life.

'Storyteller' (episode 138)
A snapshot of the dark and disturbing fantasy world that Andrew Wells inhabits as he attempts to film a video diary about the Slayer and her friends.

'Earshot' (episode 52)
The blood of a slain demon allows Buffy to gain the telepathic ability to hear the thoughts of others. But she gets far more than she bargained for.

'Prophecy Girl' (episode 12)
Buffy discovers that it is prophesied she will die in her next battle with The Master.

'Becoming' Parts 1 and 2 (episodes 33/34)
Angelus's plan to raise the demon Acathla and initiate the apocalypse forces Buffy to form a dangerous alliance and face the fact that, in order to save the world, she must kill the only man she has ever loved.

'Lies My Parents Told Me' (episode 139)
Robin Wood and Giles plan to eliminate the danger that Spike poses, but for vastly different reasons.

'A New Man' (episode 68)
Giles is turned into a demon by a devious Ethan Rayne and must convince his friends that rumours of his death have been greatly exaggerated.

'Pangs' (episode 64)
A Native American vengeance spirit attacks UC Sunnydale campus at Thanksgiving. Angel is there too, trying to help and stay out of Buffy's way at the same time.

'This Year's Girl'/'Who Are You?' (episodes 71/72)
Faith comes out of a year-long coma and initiates a fiendishly complex body-swap scenario with Buffy.

'The Zeppo' (episode 47)
Xander spends a very odd night maturing. Unfortunately, his friends are too busy to notice as they are stopping the world from ending.

'School Hard' (episode 15)
Spike leads a massive vampire attack on Sunnydale High's Parent/Teacher night.

'Phases' (episode 27)
Oz discovers that he's a werewolf and tries to avoid both Willow finding out and becoming a game hunter's latest catch.

'Angel' (episode 7)
Buffy discovers that Angel is really a vampire, while Angel himself must face his sire, Darla.

'Checkpoint' (episode 90)
The Council of Watchers come to Sunnydale to check up on what Giles has been up to since they sacked him.

'Homecoming' (episode 39)
Buffy challenges Cordelia in a beauty pageant just as Mr Trick arranges an inventive game of death for the Slayer.

'Welcome to the Hellmouth' (episode 1)
Buffy Summers arrives in Sunnydale. But she is no ordinary sixteen-year-old schoolgirl.

'Surprise'/'Innocence' (episodes 25/26)

After the interruption of her birthday party by vampires, Buffy and Angel spend the night together – something which has apocalyptic consequences for both of them.

WELL, *THAT* SUCKS!!!:
The seven worst episodes of
Buffy the Vampire Slayer

... And then, sadly, there are those handful of episodes that you would gladly *hide* on a desert island to avoid ever having to see again.

Bad Eggs (episode 24)
Two comedy vampires (who aren't, actually, in the slightest bit funny) arrive in town but fail to interact with anyone of significance as everyone is involved in a massively convoluted plot concerning demon-eggs. Actually *worse* than it sounds. There are only two rules in *Buffy* fandom – One: You will not like 'Bad Eggs'. Two: You will obey *all* the rules.

'Dead Things' (episode 113)
An episode which appears to suggest that bullied nerdish schoolboys with an interest in SF and comics will, as an inevitable consequence of the torture inflicted on them, turn into murdering rapists. Not big, not clever and not any good.

'Beer Bad' (episode 61)
Heavy-handed metaphor episode #1: Drinking beer turns men into savages.

'Beauty and the Beasts' (episode 38)
Heavy-handed metaphor episode #2: All men are savages *anyway*.

'Where the Wild Things Are' (episode 74)
Heavy-handed metaphor episode #3: All sex is dirty.

'Anne' (episode 35)
Heavy-handed metaphor episode #4: The Big City depersonalises its inhabitants.

'Help' (episode 126)
Heavy-handed metaphor episode #5: Being a teenager is horrible and the only way you can express your feelings is through really pretentious poetry. Easily the most overrated episode of the show, and 45 minutes of my life that I'll never get back again ...

I JUST *LOVE* YOUR ACCENT:
15 more-or-less accurate Britishisms in *Buffy*

Sad to report, the history of American television's perception of Britain isn't filled with accurate and realistic presentations of the British way of life. Look at those horribly clichéd *Friends* episodes set in London, for example. Or that *X-Files* featuring Mulder's Oxford girlfriend. It's all stereotypical tea-drinking, fog, red buses, beefeaters and two basic character types: snooty Lord Something-or-other, or Dick Van Dyke in *Mary Poppins*. That, plus a complete inability to pronounce the word Tottenham correctly. It was something of a relief, therefore, that *Buffy* could boast three reasonably realistic portrayals of British characters. Even Wesley, who had his detractors, managed to accurately represent one facet of the English abroad. Then, in Season 7, Molly came along and spoiled everything that had been achieved so far ...

Profane language: The final three years of *Buffy* creator Joss Whedon's education were spent in England, at Winchester Public School. Already a committed Anglophile, the experience cemented Joss's feelings and, as a bonus, taught him lots of 'dirty words that Americans don't know'.

- Thus, *Buffy*, via Giles, Spike and Wesley, single-handedly introduced bollocks, bugger, wanker, shag, pillock, knack-ered, twerp, berk, sodding, poof, etc. to a mainstream US audience. And people will *still* try to tell you that Buffy isn't a *cultural* show ...

- The series even made a joke of this – in 'Tabula Rasa' – when an amnesiac Spike sneers at Giles's obvious Britishness, then realises that he himself is English and reels off a string of expletives as proof.

On a slightly related note, Spike's silent two-fingered reply to Xander's accusation in 'Hush' that the vampire is responsible for his inability to speak is *very* British. Amusingly, this gesture has turned up on a list of 'Obscure Cultural References' on a *Buffy* Internet newsgroup.

Spike's use of the word 'bint' ('The Harsh Light of Day', 'Out of my Mind', 'Crush', 'As You Were'): This extremely derogatory (and borderline racist) term for a young woman was first used by British servicemen in the Middle East. (It derives from the Arabic word meaning 'daughter of'.) 'I *love* writing for both Spike and Giles,' scriptwriter Jane Espenson once noted, although she confessed, 'I find that I've exhausted my supply of British slang. I [must] read more *Professionals* fanfic, that's where I find [many of] the words.' *That* explains so much.

Principal Flutie refers to the British royal family and to 'all kinds of problems' in the UK ('The Harvest'). Really? Wish we had a crime rate as low as California, mate.

Xander asks if the Sunnydale High Career Day was sponsored by the British soccer-fan association ... which shows that Mr Harris knows as much about the complexities of a serious social phenomenon as he does about everything else ('What's My Line?' Part 2). And, for the last time, it's *football*. Only *Americans* call it soccer.

Spike says that he likes dog racing and Manchester United. With regard to the latter, he's somewhat typical as most of their supporters live *anywhere* but Manchester ('Becoming' Part 2).

Giles gets flustered when Gwendolyn Post arrives as Faith's new Watcher ('Revelations'). Gwendolyn suggests that there is talk within the Council of Watchers that Giles has become too American. She also uses lots of supposedly (i.e. not in the slightest) British expressions like 'everything's gone to Hell in a hand-basket' and shares Giles's obsession with tea.

Wesley informs Buffy that the three most important words for a Slayer are 'preparation, preparation, preparation' ('Bad Girls'). This could refer to a famous Tony Blair speech during 1997 in which the incumbent Prime Minister noted that the three most important things in Britain were 'education, education, education'.

One of the universities that accepts Willow's application is Oxford ('Choices'). That's where they make Gileses, notes Buffy. Of course, if *Inspector Morse* is to be believed, the town has a mortality rate even higher than Sunnydale.

In 'A New Man', Spike refers to 'a few bob', which was, no doubt, understood by about four people in the US and no one in Britain under the age of 35. For the uninitiated, a bob is a pre-decimalisation slang term for one shilling (that's twelve old pence or five new pence).

When members of the Council of Watchers arrive in Sunnydale ('Checkpoint'), Tara says that she believed the English were gentler than other people.

- Xander notes that if the Council deport Giles, as threatened, they're condemning him to a lifetime diet of blood sausage and bangers and mash. (In 'Lessons', when Willow and Giles are in the rural splendour of a wet June afternoon in Wiltshire, Willow also refers to bangers and mash – a bland sausage and potato dinner.)

- One has to admire the way in which the Council throw everyone out of The Magic Box. They're so terribly English about it, apologising to shoppers for any inconvenience caused.

In 'All the Way', Spike uses the slang phrase 'nick', meaning 'to steal'. When Xander and Anya announce their engagement, Giles notes that, where he comes from, this sort of thing requires much in the way of libation. Except we don't normally call a night out on the razzle *that*. 'God save the Queen', toasts Xander. The Sex Pistols' version, one would hope.

Spike uses the term 'sack of hammers' to describe Drusilla's mental instability. It sounds like a plausible cockney slang expression for madness, however neither *Cassell's Rhyming Slang* nor *The Oxford Dictionary of Slang* features the phrase ('Selfless').

'Sleeper' includes some painfully obvious stock-footage of London (verily, yonder, is this a red telephone box I see before me?). But we'll forgive the production this minor indiscretion since it's mercifully brief.

The arrival of Molly ('Bring On the Night') is where it all threatened to go pear-shaped. How many girls born in England during the 1980s do readers know with that particular Christian name? No, not 1870s west-country serving wenches, but girls born when the most popular female names in the country included Tiffany and Kylie. She also uses

27

several desperately out-of-date slang British terms (like 'brill', for example). Thankfully, she's killed in 'Touched', thus bringing to an end *Buffy*'s least imaginative stumble into Britishisms.

THE GOOD BOOK

Biblical references or allusions in *Buffy* include:

- Noah's Ark from Genesis 6 ('The Pack')

- Psalms 8:2 ('Angel', 'Villains')

- Isaiah 11:6 ('Prophecy Girl')

- King Solomon from 1 Chronicles ('What's My Line?' Part 1)

- 1 Corinthians 13:11 ('Faith, Hope and Trick')

- Revelations 15:1 ('Hush')

- 1 Kings: 16:21 ('Where the Wild Things Are')

- Genesis 7:15 ('Flooded')

- 1 Timothy 6:12 ('Once More, With Feeling', 'Bring On the Night')

- Genesis 1:1 ('Lessons')

- Proverbs 24:6 ('Never Leave Me')

- Matthew 6:23 ('First Date')

- Revelations 17 ('Dirty Girls')

- 1 Corinthians 12 ('Dirty Girls')

- Mark 14 ('Dirty Girls')

- Genesis 2–4 ('Dirty Girls')

- Matthew 6 ('Dirty Girls')

- Luke 15 ('Touched')

- Exodus 21 ('End of Days')

668 – THE NEIGHBOUR OF THE BEAST:
A selection of those really important Sunnydale addresses

🖐 1630 Revello Drive, Sunnydale, CA 95037: Joyce, Buffy and, subsequently, Dawn Summers' residence. And, at various times, also the home of Willow, Tara, Spike, Faith and numerous potential Slayers. As Buffy once idly wonders when the telephone rings, who could possibly be calling her – everyone she knows *lives* at her home ('Flooded').

🖐 Sunnydale's zip code, incidentally, is the real code for the town of Morgan Hill at the southern end of the Santa Clara Valley, south of San Francisco.

🖐 Building #4616: The street name on which Rupert Giles's fashionable apartment is situated is not known, but it is, seemingly, in a quiet part of town. Giles's neighbours appear to be the sort of people who don't ask too many questions about the comings and goings of young people at all hours. Or, for that matter:

- The blond gentleman who was tied up in Mr Giles's bathroom.

- That time when a demon ran amok there ('A New Man').

- The occasion when a bunch of army types turned up with tracking devices ('The I in Team').

31

They probably *do* gossip a bit about the woman's body that was found in Giles's bedroom, however (*Passion*).

 In 'Him', we discover that Xander's stylish bachelor apartment is No. 22 and that Anya's chick-pad is No. 24 (though, presumably, *not* in the same building).

 The Magic Box, 5124 Maple Court: Your one-stop shop for all your occult needs ('Shadow').

 Willow and Buffy's college accommodation was Room 214 in Stevenson Hall, at the University of California, Sunnydale ('The Freshman', 'Living Conditions').

• Riley Finn, Forrest Gates and Graham Miller were based in Lowell House.

• Maggie Walsh and The Initiative were based *under* Lowell House.

• Other dorms buildings on the UC Sunnydale campus include Fischer, Richmond, Weisman, Kresge and Porter.

 The Sunnydale telephone directory includes:

• Buffy's extension at Sunnydale High: (803) 555-0101

• The Magic Box: (803) 555-8966

• Sunnydale Docks: (803) 555-FISH

• Dawn's cellphone number is (803) 555-0193

• Xander's work number is (803) 555-0148

Other general geographical information about Sunnydale: Oxnard, California – where Xander spent the summer after graduation – is forty miles southeast. The Bronze is on the edge of town while the University of Sunnydale is located five miles from the town centre.

Sunnydale also has numerous abandoned warehouses (including the factory in which Spike, Dru and Angelus lived), located ten blocks northeast of The Bronze, The Fish Tank and Willy's Bar, which are all situated in the same part of town as the warehouse district.

The Sunnydale Armoury is ten blocks east of the town centre. Sunnydale beach can be reached off the I-17 by municipal bus #13. Sunnydale Ice Rink is on the I-17 (municipal bus #66) but, seemingly, in the opposite direction from the beach.

SCREAM A LITTLE SCREAM FOR ME

Classic horror movies referenced or alluded to in *Buffy* include:

- *The Exorcist* ('Teacher's Pet', 'I Only Have Eyes For You', 'Conversations With Dead People', 'Bring On the Night')

- *The Silence of the Lambs* ('The Pack')

- *The Shining* ('The Puppet Show', 'Bewitched, Bothered and Bewildered', 'Gone', 'Conversations With Dead People')

- *Rosemary's Baby* ('Nightmares')

- *The Bad Seed* ('Dead Man's Party')

- *Single White Female* ('Faith, Hope and Trick')

- *Marathon Man* ('Revelations')

- *Scanners* ('Lover's Walk')

- *Carrie* ('The Prom')

- *Phantasm* ('Fear Itself')

- *The Omen* ('The Gift')

- *Night of the Living Dead* ('Bargaining' Part 1)

- *The Fury* ('Bargaining' Part 1)

- *The Blair Witch Project* ('Flooded', 'Bring On the Night')

- *The Thing* ('Gone', 'Showtime')

- *Children of the Corn* ('Older and Far Away')

- *Hellraiser* ('Conversations With Dead People')

- *From Hell* ('Lies My Parents Told Me')

- *Sleepy Hollow* ('Touched')

'WE CAN DO THIS THE HARD WAY, OR ...
ACTUALLY, THERE'S *JUST* THE HARD WAY':
Eight great lines of dialogue from *Buffy*'s Season 1

Xander, on facing one's fears: 'I laugh in the face of danger. Then I hide until it goes away.' – 'The Witch'

Giles, when Buffy complains that she cannot patrol as she has a date: 'I'll just jump in my time machine, go back to the twelfth century and ask the vampires to postpone their ancient prophecy for a few days whilst you take in dinner and a show.' – 'Never Kill a Boy on the First Date'

Giles, when told by Buffy that Xander has been teasing the less fortunate, has a noticeable change in demeanour and is spending his time lounging about: 'It's devastating. He's turned into a sixteen-year-old boy. Of course, you'll have to kill him.' – 'The Pack'

Willow, on the concept of telling the truth: 'That way lies madness, and sweaty palms.' – 'Angel'

Jenny, to Giles: 'I know our ways are strange to you, but soon you will join us in the twentieth century, with three whole years to spare.' – 'I, Robot ... You, Jane'

Snyder's mission statement: 'There are things I will not tolerate. Students loitering on campus after school. Horrible murders with hearts being removed. And also, smoking.' – 'The Puppet Show'

Buffy's mission statement, to Giles: 'I think I speak for everyone here when I say "*Huh?*"' – 'Out of Mind, Out of Sight'

Willow, on finding dead bodies at school: 'It wasn't our world any more. They [the vampires] made it theirs. And they had *fun*.' – 'Prophecy Girl'

Songs to sing and learn:
17 great musical moments from The Bronze
(… and other Sunnydale locations)

Described by Willow as the coolest place in Sunnydale (not that it has a great deal of competition) and by Cordelia as 'the scene', The Bronze club has witnessed many great musical performances over the years. One or two of them have even managed to conclude *before* being rudely interrupted by a vampire attack. Judging from Aimee Mann's throwaway comments in 'Sleeper', the club's rowdy reputation seems to have spread far beyond Sunnydale's city limits. But, curiously, bands still play there …

Superfine's 'Already Met You' ('Teacher's Pet'). The singer seems less than impressed with Xander's 'I've just stepped on an electric wire' dancing.

Velvet Chain's dramatic rendition of 'Strong' ('Never Kill a Boy on the First Date').

Cibo Matto, featuring Sean Lennon, and their performance of 'Spoon' and 'Sugar Water' ('When She Was Bad').

Dingoes Ate My Baby's classic – if arbitrarily censored – anthem 'Pain' ('Bewitched, Bothered and Bewildered'). The Dingoes, with Oz on guitar and Devon on vocals, appear in many episodes and seem to be – for a while, at least – The

Bronze's resident house band. Their songs were, in reality, provided by the band Four Star Mary.

🎺 The beautiful 'Virgin State of Mind' performed by K's Choice ('Doppelgängland').

🎺 Bif Naked's 'Moment of Weakness', 'Anything' and the epic 'Lucky' ('The Harsh Light of Day'). This performance actually took place not in The Bronze but at a party on the UC Sunnydale campus, which Buffy attended with the loathsome Parker Abrams.

🎺 Shy, featuring vocals by the seductive Veruca, playing 'Dip' and 'Need To Destroy' ('Wild At Heart'). They also appear in 'Beer Bad'. Their music was actually provided by the band THC. George Sarah, THC's composer/programmer, appears as Shy's keyboard player.

🎺 Jonathan Levinson's Sinatra-esque rendition of 'Serenade in Blue' ('Superstar'). In reality, Royal Crown Revue are the band and Brad Kane provided the vocals for Danny Strong to mime to.

🎺 Rupert Giles's beautiful version of Pete Townshend's 'Behind Blue Eyes' at the Espresso Pump ('Where the Wild Things Are'). That really *is* Tony Head singing, although the guitar was played by *Buffy*'s musical supervisor, John King.

🎺 Anthony Stewart Head (vocals), Christophe Beck (piano) and Four Star Mary (all other instruments) performing Joss Whedon's downright peculiar 'The Exposition Song' ('Restless').

🎺 Man of the Year's 'Just As Nice' ('All the Way').

🥊 Michelle Branch's gorgeous rendition of 'Goodbye to You' ('Tabula Rasa').

🥊 Grunge rockers Virgil perform fierce versions of 'Vermillion Borders', 'Parachute' and 'Here' ('Smashed'). When a recently de-ratted Amy and Willow get bored with events and do some prestidigitation, the group are, briefly and magically, replaced by the girl band Halo Friendlies doing a cracking version of 'Run Away'.

🥊 At *last*, a bona fide chart band play The Bronze: The Breeders performing 'Little Fury' and 'Son of Three' ('Him').

🥊 Angie Heart, of series favourites Splendid, singing 'Blue' ('Conversations With Dead People'). Splendid had previously appeared in both 'I Only Have Eyes For You' and 'The Freshman'. The band's guitarist, Jesse Tobias, helped Joss Whedon and Chris Beck arrange the songs in the musical episode 'Once More, With Feeling'. He also appeared with Michelle Branch, for whom he's musical director.

🥊 Aimee Mann performs 'Pavlov's Bell' and 'This Is How It Goes' ('Sleeper'), and, as a bonus, has one of the best lines of dialogue in the episode.

🥊 What kind of band plays The Bronze during an apocalypse? asks Kennedy. Actually, they're Nerf Herder, whose manic 'Buffy Theme' features at the start of every episode. It's fitting, perhaps, that the last time we see a band playing the club it's them performing 'Rock City News' and 'Mr Spock' ('Empty Places').

BEWITCHED:

Five Willow Rosenberg spells that didn't have anything like the desired effect

Willow was first attracted to dabbling in the dark arts due to the influence of her techno-pagan teacher, Jenny Calendar. Willow soon became highly proficient in witchcraft and has, on many occasions, used her powers to help Buffy against some dangerous enemies. On occasions, however, she gets it all disastrously wrong.

'Gingerbread': Condemned by the possessed townsfolk as witches, Buffy, Willow and Amy Madison are to be burned at the stake (let's ignore, for a moment, the folly of holding a witch-burning *indoors*). Amy casts a spell and turns herself into a rat to escape a fiery death. Willow, subsequently, spends the next three years attempting to reverse the spell – albeit managing it, momentarily, in 'Something Blue' – before coming up with a permanent solution ('Smashed').

'Doppelgängland': Willow is upset with Buffy and Xander, who, she feels, take her for granted (she even gives herself a mocking nickname, Reliable Dog-Geyser Person). She is, therefore, pleased when Anya Jenkins, the new girl in school, asks for Willow's help in retrieving her mother's lost amulet. However, for a variety of reasons the retrieval spell is compromised, the result being the summoning from another dimension of a vampire Willow doppelgänger.

41

'Something Blue': Traumatised by the departure of Oz, Willow is further dismayed that her pain is being patronised or misunderstood by her friends. She casts a spell which, she believes, will help. But, inadvertently, she makes all of her wishes come true. So, when she angrily suggests that Buffy and Spike should get married, or that Xander is a sexual magnet for demons, or that Giles is blind, that's *exactly* what happens.

'Once More, With Feeling'/'Tabula Rasa': Having had an argument with Tara over Willow's growing dependence on magic as a cure-all ('All the Way'), Willow casts a spell to make Tara forget that they were arguing. Tara subsequently discovers this and challenges Willow to go a week without using magic. Needless to say, an addicted Willow is unable to do so. Grief-stricken over her stupidity in resurrecting Buffy from paradise ('Bargaining' Part 1), Willow creates a spell to make Buffy forget. Instead, the spell goes awry and causes all of the Scooby Gang to wake up with amnesia.

'Same Time, Same Place': Having recently returned to Sunnydale, Willow's attempts to perform a locator spell to find the demon who has flayed the skin from its victim is unsuccessful and only succeeds in setting fire to Anya's new carpet.

'YOU MAY REMEMBER ME FROM SUCH FILMS AND TV SHOWS AS ...':
15 somewhat familiar guest stars on *Buffy*

Jean Speegle Howard (the real Natalie French in 'Teacher's Pet') was the mother of director Ron Howard and had a memorable role in his movie *Apollo 13* as Jim Lovell's confused mom.

Clea DuVall (the psychotic Marcie Ross in 'Out of Mind, Out of Sight') played Stokely Mitchell in *The Faculty*.

Jason Behr (the doomed Billy Fordham in 'Lie To Me') would, subsequently, star as the alien schoolboy, Max Evans, in *Roswell*.

The late John Ritter (the eponymous evil android in 'Ted') was a well-known sitcom star from *Three's Company* (the US version of *Man About The House*).

Willie Garson (the security guard whom Cordelia seduces in 'Killed By Death') features in such movies as *There's Something About Mary*, *Mars Attack!*, *Groundhog Day* and *The Rock*, and the TV series *Stargate SG-1*.

Jennifer Hetrick (Ms Mason in 'Homecoming') was Captain Picard's sometime girlfriend, Vash, in *Star Trek: The Next Generation*.

Serena Scott Thomas (the duplicitous Gwendolyn Post in 'Revelations') played James Bond's extremely sexy doctor in *The World is Not Enough*.

Jeff Kober (the insane Kralik in 'Helpless' and the warlock Rack in 'Wrecked') was Ray, the voice of Reef Radio, in those annoying Bacardi adverts and also featured in a particularly memorable *X-Files* episode, 'Ice'.

Lindsay Crouse (Professor Maggie Walsh in 'The Freshman') played Kate McBride in *Hill Street Blues*.

Kathryn Joosten (the wicked Mrs Holt in 'Where the Wild Things Are') is best remembered as President Bartlet's secretary, Mrs Landingham, in *The West Wing*.

Abraham Benrubi (Anya's troll ex-husband, Olaf, in 'Triangle') played Larry Kubiac in the cult early-90s comedy series *Parker Lewis Can't Lose* and, more recently, Jerry Markovic in *ER*.

Joel Gray (The Doc in 'Forever') won an Oscar in 1972 for his acclaimed performance as the Emcee in *Cabaret*.

Hilton Battle (Sweet in 'Once More, With Feeling') is a Broadway veteran who played the Scarecrow in *The Wiz*.

Glenn Morshower (Cassie Newton's waste-of-space father in 'Help') is one of only two men who works in the administrations of both Presidents Bartlet and Palmer, playing defence analyst Mike Chysler in *The West Wing* and Secret Service Agent Aaron Pierce in *24*. He also played Sheriff Mobley in *CSI: Crime Scene Investigation*.

Ashanti (the demonic Lissa in 'First Date') is a soul diva best known for hits such as 'Foolish', 'Always on Time' and 'What's Luv?'.

'GOD, XANDER, IS THAT *ALL* YOU THINK ABOUT?':
10 examples of Xander Harris's overcomplicated love life

Cordelia once asked Xander if looking at guns made him want to have sex. Xander replied with complete honesty that he was seventeen and even looking at *linoleum* made him want to have sex. This section, therefore, lists Alexander LaVelle Harris's problematic relationships with members of the opposite sex.

 Willow:

- Xander's first girlfriend. Willow tells Buffy in 'Welcome to the Hellmouth' that they broke up when Xander stole her Barbie doll. They were five at the time.

- They remained close friends through school, however, and there's more than one suggestion that they played naïve sexual games ('Killed By Death').

- It's obvious to everyone (with the notable exception of Xander himself) the depth of feeling that Willow maintains, which explains her hysterical reaction when discovering that he's been secretly dating Cordelia ('Innocence').

- They finally allow their attraction to flourish, briefly, in 'Homecoming' and 'Lover's Walk'.

- The trauma of losing Cordelia because of the latter indiscretion seems to finally wake Xander up to the fact that he and Willow aren't meant to be with each other.

- Willow's subsequent discovery that she's gay ('The I in Team', 'Goodbye Iowa') is the final nail in that particular coffin.

 Buffy:

- Xander gives Buffy a wrist-chain with the words ALWAYS YOURS engraved on it. He *claims* that it came that way ('The Witch').

- Xander asks Buffy to the prom and is, politely, rejected ('Prophecy Girl').

- He continues to burn a torch for Buffy long afterwards (see, for example, 'Surprise' and his fantasy of a millionaire Xander saving Buffy from a loveless relationship with Angel).

- With maturity, however, comes a realisation that Buffy, like Willow, is meant to be Xander's best friend but never his girlfriend.

- In the college years, Xander becomes Buffy's confidante ('The Freshman'), her confessor and the person to whom she entrusts her most important tasks (like taking Dawn away from Sunnydale in 'End of Days').

 Amy Madison:

- There's no direct indication that Amy and Xander dated but Xander's use of blackmail to get Amy to perform a spell in 'Bewitched, Bothered and Bewildered' suggests a familiarity with each other that goes beyond mere classmates.

- When Willow tells a rehumanised Amy that Xander is getting married to a millennium-aged capitalist ex-demon with rabbit-phobia ('Smashed'), Amy huffily replies, 'That's *so* his type,' indicating that she knows what his type *is* ... and, perhaps, that she wasn't it.

 Joyce:

- Along with all the other women in Sunnydale, Joyce is attracted to Xander when Amy casts the love spell on him in 'Bewitched, Bothered and Bewildered'.

- Xander's dream in 'Restless' suggests that such naughty and, frankly, *wrong* feelings might not be entirely the stuff of bad magic.

 Cordelia:

- Even though Xander was once the treasurer of the *We Hate Cordelia Club*, when Xander and Cordy are trapped in Buffy's basement by Mister Pfister ('What's My Line?' Part 2) their hormones *explode*.

- After a few weeks of secretive necking in closets and behind the library bookshelves, they allow their lustful exuberance (which, Willow disgustedly notes, is against all laws of God and man) to become public.

- Cordy suffers the ridicule of her friends, particularly Harmony ('Bewitched, Bothered and Bewildered').

- Xander's friends, on the other hand, are baffled: Willow tells Buffy that Xander's new phone number is 1-800-I'm-Dating-A-Skanky-Ho ('Phases').

- Xander and Cordy's relationship survives Xander almost becoming an aquatic monster ('Go Fish').

- Cordelia battling Buffy in a popularity contest ('Homecoming').

- But it comes to a shattering end in 'Lover's Walk'.

- Xander and Cordy then spend the following months scoring cheap points at each other's expense, before Xander proves that he's a bigger man than anyone suspected, buying Cordy's prom dress when she encounters financial difficulties.

- Cordelia's relocation to Los Angeles prevents any chance of them becoming attached again.

It's clear that Xander, like Chandler in *Friends*, is regarded by many – and, perhaps, even secretly by himself – as a closet gay:

- He's witty (frequently in a self-deprecating way), knows way too much about popular culture, is *lousy* with women (even though his best friends are all girls) and his dates usually go disastrously wrong. (Lysette – 'The Zeppo' – is purely interested in his car.)

- Only his less-than-immaculate taste in clothes suggests that Xander hasn't taken all of his gay exams yet.

- His inadvertent outing of Larry ('Phases'), and Larry's subsequent transformation into a decent, likeable human being by the experience, is significant.

- Xander is, as a consequence, in obvious denial about his own latent sexual identity. (Most clearly seen in 'Earshot', although also in conversations with Andrew in Season 7, particularly one in 'First Date' regarding *Enterprise* star Scott Bakula.)

 It is, perhaps, for this reason that many of Xander's dates have been with predatory females who have something supernaturally wrong with them. These include:

- The She-Mantis, Ms French ('Teacher's Pet')

- The seductive Ampata ('Inca Mummy Girl')

- Anya ('The Prom')

- Lissa ('First Date')

 If we take this to extremely Freudian levels, the fact that, in Cordelia's wish-universe, Xander is a vampire and, therefore, also dead, suggests that *she* wants to kill him as well.

 Faith:

- Xander loses his virginity during one of the most absurd nights of his life ('The Zeppo'). The ridiculousness of his liaison is emphasised when, after a riotous – if brief – session, he's pushed out of Faith's motel room with his pants in his hands and a confused look on his face. Yeah, man, we've *all* had those sort of nights …

- 'Consequences' establishes Faith's BDSM credentials (alluded to again in 'Dirty Girls'). Xander appears less than keen on autoerotic asphyxiation.

- That Faith still holds *marginally* fond memories of these events is apparent – she tells Amanda and Kennedy that she uses the fact she had Xander first to shut Anya up ('Empty Places').

 Anya:

- Though asked to the prom by Anya simply because he wasn't as objectionable as the other alpha males ('The Prom'), their relationship really began when they had sex for the first time ('The Harsh Light of Day'). It seemed, initially, that mutual admiration of Xander's penis was pretty much all they had in common, but the relationship survived:
  - Xander acquiring mystical syphilis ('Pangs').
  - The inconvenience of Spike moving into Xander's apartment ('Hush').
  - A flirtation with sadomasochism ('The I in Team').
  - A possible case of erectile dysfunction ('Where the Wild Things Are').
  - Xander's erotic dreams ('Restless').
  - Xander being split into two bodies ('The Replacement').
  - The return of Anya's ex ('Triangle').

- During this period, Xander finally proposed to Anya and, once the world hadn't ended, the couple formally announced their intention to marry ('All the Way'). Though some well-hidden doubts in both of their minds emerged during 'Once More, With Feeling'.

- It was for this reason, rather than the machinations of one of Anya's former victims, that Xander left his bride waiting at the alter in 'Hell's Bell'.

- With Anya returning to D'Hoffryn's vengeance-demon brigade, a miserable Xander tried to apologise to his former love.

- His explanations, however, were rejected and it wasn't until Andrew confronted the pair a year later ('Storyteller') that they finally got to the root of their problem.

- Subsequently, the couple had some fantastic break-up sex, agreeing that it felt like a 'one last time'-style situation.

- However, see 'Touched' for an utterly superb encore.

- Anya's heroic death in 'Chosen' leaves Xander clearly heartbroken.

Post Anya, Xander had a few isolated dates. But most seemed to go disastrously wrong – see, for example, Nancy ('Beneath You'), abandoned due to an attack of a worm-monster. It's sad, really – Xander's a good-looking lad, a loyal and true friend, not to mention a skilled craftsman; he should have women flocking around him. By the end of the series, however, he's a visually challenged, unemployed, homeless carpenter who still has erotic dreams about teenage nymphets ('Dirty Girls').

'I WISH DATING WAS LIKE SLAYING. SIMPLE, DIRECT, STAKE TO THE HEART':
12 great lines of dialogue from *Buffy*'s Season 2

Giles, on American football: 'It's rather odd that a nation that prides itself on its virility should feel compelled to strap on forty pounds of protective gear in order to play rugby.' – 'Some Assembly Required'

Spike gives vampirism a historical context: 'If every vampire who said he was at the crucifixion was actually there, it would've been like Woodstock.' – 'School Hard'

Cordelia's reaction to Willow telling her that she isn't a cat, she's in high school, and that they are her friends – well, sort of ...: 'That's nice, Willow. And you went mental *when* ...?' – 'Halloween'

Giles lies to Buffy: 'The bad guys are easily distinguished by their pointy horns or black hats; we always defeat them and save the day. No one ever dies and everybody lives happily ever after.' – 'Lie To Me'

Xander's moment of Premier League sarcasm: 'A bonus day at class, plus Cordelia? Mix in a little rectal surgery and it's *my best day ever*.' – 'The Dark Age'

Giles, when one of Buffy's rants changes focus halfway through: 'I believe the subtext here is rapidly becoming the text.' – 'Ted'

Willow, angry at discovering Xander and Cordelia kissing: 'I *knew* it. Well, knew it in the sense of not having the slightest idea. But I *knew* there was something I didn't know.' – 'Innocence'

Cain: 'First they tell me I can't hunt an elephant for its ivory. Now I've got to deal with People for the Ethical Treatment of Werewolves.' – 'Phases'

Xander, when Buffy suggests that they should comfort each other: 'Would lap dancing enter into that scenario at all? 'Cause I find that *very* comforting.' – 'Bewitched, Bothered and Bewildered'

Angel's words of wisdom: 'If we could live without passion, maybe we'd know some kind of peace. But we'd be hollow. Empty rooms, shuttered and dank. Without passion, we'd be truly dead.' – 'Passion'

Cordelia, when believing that Xander had become an aquatic monster: 'We can still date … or not. I'd understand if you want to see other fish.' – 'Go Fish'

Buffy, to Angel's mentor Whistler: 'If you're gonna crack jokes, I'm going to pull out your ribcage and wear it as a hat.' – 'Becoming' Part 2

DON'T BE IN THE TEASER:

20 reasons why, if you're going to be in a *Buffy* episode, it may be an idea to avoid the pre-title sequence

Supernaturally terrible things seem to happen to Sunnydale residents with alarming regularity in those vital few moments between the 'Previously on *Buffy the Vampire Slayer* ...' recap and the actual title sequence itself. This section lists some of the most memorable.

'Welcome to the Hellmouth': A former student of Sunnydale High breaks into the school with his girlfriend. Unfortunately for him, she is, in reality, not a petrified school-girl, but rather a 500-year-old vampiress named Darla. Once he establishes that there's no one around, he's history.

'The Witch': Amber Grove bursts into flames during try-outs in what is, surely, the first recorded case of Spontaneous Cheerleader Combustion.

'Teacher's Pet': Sympathetic biology professor Dr Gregory is dragged into a supply cupboard and eaten by a giant-sized She-Mantis. That's no way to treat a colleague.

'The Pack': In the Hyena House of Sunnydale Zoo, some-thing supernaturally nasty happens to Xander and the school's resident bully-kids Kyle, Rhonda, Tor and Heidi.

✊ 'I, Robot … You, Jane': Cortona, Italy, 1418. Carlo, a young man, has his neck broken by Moloch, a horned, green-skinned corrupter demon. An incantation known as The Circle of Kayless subsequently traps Moloch's essence within the pages of a book.

✊ 'The Puppet Show': Changing in the dressing room after her dance performance at rehearsals for the Sunnydale High Talent Show, Emily is attacked by something with mono-chrome vision. It tells her, in a guttural voice, that it will be flesh. Then it rips out her heart.

✊ 'Reptile Boy': Buffy, Xander and Willow are watching a Hindi movie on television – the plot seems to involve a woman who's sad because the wizard cut open the bag of salt and now the dancing minions have nowhere to put their big maypole fish-thing. Meanwhile, a young woman named Cally jumps from a first-storey window and tries to escape from a pursuing group of robed figures. Inevitably, she fails.

✊ 'Innocence': Angel, having enjoyed a moist moment of happiness with Buffy, goes outside into the even more moist raging thunderstorm. He falls to the ground. Then he gets up, his soul gone, and takes the opportunity for a first decent meal in *years*.

✊ 'Go Fish': At a beach party for the victorious Sunnydale High swim team, one of the swimmers, Dodd, hears strange noises from the ocean. Then, without warning, he sheds his skin and becomes an aquatic monster, leaving behind only the steaming tattooed flesh of his former body.

✊ 'Faith, Hope and Trick': A teenager working at the Happy Burger drive-thru takes the newly arrived Mr Trick's order of a diet soda when the vampire's stretch limo pulls up to his window. While waiting for his drink, Mr Trick discusses Sunnydale's pros and cons with his master, Kakistos. Then, the teenager finds *himself* on the menu as a snack for the now-ravenous vampire.

'The Wish': Buffy struggles with an Octopoid-faced demon while Xander and Willow desperately search for something with which to kill it. Having done so, the trio then look forward to the forthcoming joys of burying the creature.

'Gingerbread': Accompanying Buffy on cemetery patrol, Joyce (complete with a Thermos flask) wanders off while Buffy is engaged in a life-and-death struggle with Mr Sanderson from the bank. Joyce finds the bodies of two small children in a nearby playground. But, as ever in Sunnydale, things are not always what they seem.

'Graduation Day' Part 1: Professor Lester Worth, a renowned vulcanology expert, is (Mayor Wilkins believes) a possible threat to his forthcoming ascension. So he sends Faith to kill the professor, which she does, ruthlessly, with her new knife.

'Where the Wild Things Are': Buffy and Riley face off against an unusual combination – a vampire/horned-demon tag-team in the cemetery. This causes Buffy to suggest that, while Riley should tackle fang, she herself will get horny. And, after killing it, she, indeed, does.

'No Place Like Home': Two months ago, somewhere in Central Europe: three monks (one wearing the worst toupee you have *ever* seen) perform a ceremony to convert the mythical energy of The Key into human flesh before they are stopped from their task by a menace that's trying to smash down their heavily barred door.

✒ 'Checkpoint': A harmless postal worker is brought to Glory's apartment by two of her minions so that the clearly distressed Glorificus can take what she needs from the man with a brain-suck.

✒ 'The Gift': In a poorly lit back alley, Buffy encounters a vampire. However, for the first time in ages, this one doesn't know who she is. Somewhat charmed by this increasingly rare occurrence, Buffy indulges in some old-school sarcasm, before staking the vampire and rescuing its intended victim.

✒ 'Smashed': Buffy interrupts what she, at first, believes to be a vampire attack on a couple. In reality, as she discovers, it's a simple mugging. Buffy prepares to give the two perpetrators the chinning of a lifetime, until Spike involves himself and the two robbers escape.

✒ 'Lessons'/'Beneath You': Two examples of foreshadowing in the Season 7 plot-arc, with two potential Slayers – one in Istanbul, the other in Frankfurt – pursued through the streets by The First's robed assassins, The Bringers. Upon capture, their potential is terminated, with extreme prejudice.

✒ 'Selfless': In a room of a UC Sunnydale frat house, the aftermath of a slaughter is visible. The blood-soaked carnage of a dozen boys lies scattered around the room – all have had their hearts ripped from their chests. In the middle of them crouches Anya, covered in blood, dazed and confused.

DENIAL, THY NAME IS JOYCE:

Five examples of Joyce Summers's uncanny ability to deliberately miss the bleeding obvious

Joyce Summers's amazing propensity for self-delusion in connection with her daughter's Slayer-related activities has become legendary. Kristine Sutherland, who played Joyce, confessed in a revealing interview, 'A parent of an adolescent has to walk a fine line, and sometimes what's called for is a healthy dose of denial and looking the other way.' And that's exactly what Joyce does for two years. When she finally discovers Buffy's secret – in 'Becoming' Part 2 – Joyce asks if Buffy has tried *not* being a Slayer. Buffy rages at her mother's inability to see what has been staring her in the face, asking how many times Joyce has washed blood out of Buffy's clothes and never asked any questions. Here are some of Joyce's more outrageous 'don't ask, don't tell' moments:

Joyce believes that the neck wounds she received when Darla bit her were caused by her fainting and falling on a barbecue fork … despite the fact that she doesn't, actually, own one ('Angel').

Even by her own standards, some sort of award is due to Joyce for even *thinking* about believing Ted's story about him simply *not* having died after Buffy pushed him down the stairs ('Ted').

How could Joyce fall for Cordelia's Scavenger Hunt excuse in reply to the screamingly obvious question, 'What are you twenty girls and one boy doing in my basement and why am I holding a carving knife?' ('Bewitched, Bothered and Bewildered'). Since everyone affected by Amy's love spell seems to have retained at least some of their memories of these events afterwards, it is reasonable to assume that this also applied to Joyce and that she is, as Buffy suggests, repressing after hitting on Xander.

Joyce states – in 'Anne' – that she doesn't blame herself for Buffy leaving Sunnydale. Instead, she blames Giles. That's pretty hypocritical since it was Joyce who threw Buffy out of the house in the first place.

Having had sex with Giles (twice) on the hood of a police car when infected by demonic chocolates ('Band Candy'), Joyce spends the next few episodes avoiding contact with Giles wherever possible. When Buffy gains telepathic abilities ('Earshot'), the truth is, amusingly, outed.

WILLIAM, IT WAS REALLY NOTHING:
The complicated psyche, lives and loves of Spike, the second vampire with a soul

Spike was introduced in 'School Hard' as a one-shot villain; based on doomed Sex Pistols bassist Sid Vicious, Spike's job was to cause havoc, crack a bunch of one-liners and then *die*. However, as with other characters who were envisioned as similarly short-lived – Wesley, Andrew and Anya, for example – Spike survived his planned exit (in 'What's My Line?' Part 2). And, after a period recuperating, formed an unlikely alliance with the Slayer to defeat Angelus. Then he roared out of town in his DeSoto unlikely to be seen again ('Becoming' Part 2). But a year later, a drunken, lovelorn Spike crashed back into Sunnydale, caused havoc, then hit the road again, leaving heartache and destruction in his wake ('Lover's Walk'). Subsequently, he returned to Sunnydale for a third time ('The Harsh Light of Day', 'Wild At Heart', 'The Initiative'). He was back to stay.

Spike's journey was compelling and more than a little twisted. He went from being the Big Bad, who, for some reason, always got his ass kicked in Sunnydale, to an annoyingly sarcastic neighbour, an uneasy ally, a (sort of) love interest – and then a would-be rapist. This was followed by a period of insanity before he finally became the repentant hero who, literally, saved the world to achieve redemption. In the process, we learned a lot about his history and his unique world-view. When Spike finally exited this mortal coil in a blaze of glory ('Chosen'), he was sincerely mourned. Not bad for a disposable villain with a dodgy haircut.

William The Bloody Awful Poet: In London, in 1880, an educated young man named William (last name unknown) was awkward and bookish with none of the later arrogant swagger. He was devoted to his ailing mother, Anne, besotted (in an unrequited way) with Cecily Underwood and poured out his broken heart into some of the worst poetry ever committed to paper.

Ill at ease in polite society ('Fool for Love'), surrounded by his alleged friends, social-climbing *nouveau riche* vulgarians, he takes their cruel, dismissive treatment with a quiet dignity and courageously admits that every syllable of his poetry is written for Cecily. Although he may be a bad poet, by contrast he's a good *man*.

Cecily's rejection of him is cold, brutal and total (as one would expect from a woman who may, in fact, be a vengeance-demon in disguise); a distraught William flees to an alley, unwittingly attracting the attention of three vampires – Angelus, Darla and Drusilla.

In death, as in life, William shows that he possesses unusual strength of character; faced with a beautiful woman who morphs into a monster, rather than running a mile William looks fascinated as Drusilla erotically sires him. (Later, he tells Buffy that dying made him feel *alive* for the first time.) William seizes his new existence with both hands and soon builds himself a reputation rivalled only by his grand sire and sometime mentor Angelus. But William The Poet is never far from the surface of Spike The Vampire.

Shaped from the pain of rejection and unrequited love, William's new persona is capable of vulnerability and affection. He never, as Drusilla notes in 'Crush', loses his capacity to love, not wisely, perhaps, but too well. And his loyalty to those he loves, both in life and death, is *total*. He is also devious, cunning, impatient, tactless, untrustworthy, terribly immature and a bit of a prat at times. All of these characterisitics are vital to understanding the vampire that Spike, ultimately, becomes.

SATURDAY NIGHT AT THE MOVIES

Classic films referenced or alluded to in *Buffy* include:

- *The Untouchables* ('Never Kill a Boy on the First Date', 'Fool for Love', 'Showtime')

- *The Usual Suspects* ('The Puppet Show')

- *The Wizard of Oz* ('The Pack', 'Nightmares', 'The Yoko Factor', 'No Place Like Home', 'Seeing Red', 'Grave', 'Empty Places')

- *Planet of the Apes* ('When She Was Bad', 'The Freshman')

- *The Godfather* ('Halloween', 'The Yoko Factor', 'Hell's Bells')

- *Thelma and Louise* ('Ted')

- *The Wild Bunch* ('Bad Eggs')

- *Dead Poets Society* ('Surprise')

- *Faster, Pussycat! Kill! Kill!* ('Passion')

- *JFK* ('I Only Have Eyes For You', 'First Date')

- *Network* ('I Only Have Eyes For You')

- *The English Patient* ('Beauty and the Beasts')

- *Apocalypse Now* ('Gingerbread', 'Restless')

- *Bill and Ted's Excellent Adventure* ('Doppelgängland')

- *Star Wars* ('Choices', 'All the Way')

- *Star Wars Episode 1: The Phantom Menace* ('The Freshman')

- *Twelve Angry Men* ('Choices')

- *Jaws* ('Graduation Day' Part 1, 'End of Days')

- *The Terminator* ('Living Conditions')

- *Fantasia* ('Fear Itself', 'All the Way')

- *Aliens* ('The I in Team')

- *The Right Stuff* ('This Year's Girl')

- *The Matrix* ('Superstar', 'Primeval', 'Touched')

- *Bull Durham* ('Buffy vs. Dracula')

- *This is Spinal Tap* ('Real Me')

- *The Graduate* ('Into the Woods', 'Him')

- *The Hunchback of Notre Dame* ('Crush')

- *Indiana Jones and the Last Crusade* ('Spiral', 'Never Leave Me')

- *Peter Pan* ('Bargaining' Part 2)

- *Mean Streets* ('After Life')

- *Groundhog Day* ('Life Serial')

- *Raiders of the Lost Ark* ('All the Way', 'Chosen')

- *Toy Story* ('All the Way')

- *Gone With The Wind* ('Tabula Rasa')

- *Hardball* ('Smashed')

- *Sleepless in Seattle* ('Doublemeat Palace')

- *Very Bad Things* ('Dead Things')

- *The Thin Man* ('As You Were')

- *Taxi Driver* ('Normal Again')

- *Blue Velvet* ('Normal Again')

- *One Flew Over the Cuckoo's Nest* ('Normal Again')

- *Thunderball* ('Seeing Red')

- *Gladiator* ('Two To Go')

- *Trading Places* ('Grave')

- *Almost Famous* ('Lessons', 'Dirty Girls')

- *Picnic At Hanging Rock* ('Lessons')

- *Run Lola Run* ('Beneath You')

- *Signs* ('Bring On the Night')

- *The Spy Who Came In From The Cold* ('Showtime')

- *Mad Max Beyond Thunderdome* ('Showtime')

- *Top Gun* ('Potential')

- *Pulp Fiction* ('Get It Done')

- *Ghostbusters* ('The Killer In Me')

- *A Hard Day's Night* ('Lies My Parents Told Me')

- *Spartacus* ('Dirty Girls')

- *Crouching Tiger, Hidden Dragon* ('Touched')

- *Excalibur* ('Touched')

- *Monty Python's Holy Grail* ('End of Days')

DREAMING, AS BLONDIE ONCE
SAID, IS FREE:
Those psychedelically mind-expanding dream
sequences in full

Lots of TV series do way-cool hallucinatory dream sequences as part of their dramatic arsenal. *Buffy*, on the other hand, does *magnificent*, surreal, scary, funny ones. You'll find the best of them listed here.

'Nightmares': Among the dreams that are made flesh when the astral projection of an abused little boy, Billy Palmer, begins to affect reality are:

- Buffy walking into The Master's lair but being powerless against him.

- She also has hidden fears concerning
  - a history test that she hasn't studied for
  - her father telling her that *she* was the real reason for her parents' divorce
  - most pointedly, being turned into a vampire herself.

- Giles's two nightmares involve losing his ability to read and Buffy's death.

- Xander also has twin fears – nakedness (except for his underwear) in class and a terrible clown who terrorised him at his sixth birthday party.

- Willow suffers from extreme stage fright.

- Cordelia has a bad-hair day and turns into a Chess Club geek.

- Wendell's arachnophobia is understandable once he explains the background to it.

- The Way-Cool Guy's worst fear is of his mom embarrassing him in front of his friends (one that we've all probably shared).

- *Come on*, who dreamed about giant flies destroying Sunnydale?

'Surprise': Like all good dreams, Buffy's in this episode features a rock'n'roll soundtrack:

- In The Bronze, Willow speaks to Buffy in French accompanied by a small monkey (a very subtle allusion to a throwaway line of Oz's in 'What's My Line?' Part 2).

- Crockery smashes and, in a moment dripping with Freudian symbolism, Angel is staked by Drusilla.

- Buffy mentions a dream that she once had in which she and Giles opened an office warehouse in Las Vegas ... which, actually, sounds like a rather good series in itself.

Three classic examples of the Buffy/Angel 'shipper-dream dynamic:

- In 'Anne', Buffy and Angel are at their most romantic, on a beach at sunset.

- 'Dead Man's Party' sees them together in a deserted school talking around the subject of Angel's death.

- In 'The Prom', Angel himself dreams that he and Buffy marry in church, walk down the aisle and out on to a beautiful sunny day, at which point she, rather than Angel, bursts into flames.

🖎 'Graduation Day' Part 2/'This Year's Girl': Buffy and Faith's seemingly shared dreams feature the two of them making a bed together in Faith's apartment and talking, in highly veiled terms (and, sometimes, in absolute riddles), about the coming arrival of Buffy's sister, Dawn. There's also a cat and a knife, which feature prominently in both.

🖎 'Restless': Dealing entirely with dreamscapes, 'Restless' is an episode about secrets. That half-hidden laughter behind closed doors and shuttered windows. Abuse-monsters, public nudity, what the future holds ... *these* are the dreams that make us. And the cheese will *not* protect us.

🖎 Willow dreams – in 'Restless' – that she's attending drama class, a surreal adaptation of *Death of a Salesman*, starring her friends, in which she doesn't know her lines.

- Her stage fright was central to both 'The Puppet Show' and 'Nightmares'. In 'The Zeppo', Willow tells Buffy that every nightmare she's ever had that doesn't involve academic failure or public nudity concerns the Hellmouth creature seen in 'Prophecy Girl'. In fact, she once dreamed it attacked her while she was late for a test *and* naked.

- Willow finds herself back in class, wearing the clothes that she wore on the day she first met Buffy, while everyone in class laughs at her, and Tara and Oz whisper behind her back.

 Xander's labyrinthine dream contains images of:

• Joyce Summers's sexuality.

• Giles, Spike and Buffy playing like children while Xander ponders his future.

• Driving his ice-cream truck with Anya and finding himself attracted to Willow and Tara.

• An inability to understand what Giles and Anya say to him.

• All of his escape attempts leading him back to his basement, where he meets Snyder – in a scene inspired by Captain Willard's meeting with Colonel Kurtz in *Apocalypse Now* – and a brutish representation of his father.

Giles dreams of himself, Olivia (pushing a pram) and a childlike Buffy at a funfair, where Spike has hired himself out as a crass public attraction.

• At The Bronze, Giles meets Willow and Xander and, while Anya performs a terrible stand-up routine, he works out what's going on, telling his friends in an exposition song.

• All of these dreams end with a savage black girl sucking the life from Willow, pulling out Xander's heart and scalping Giles. (The spirit, the heart, the mind … Remember that, it might be important.)

71

✒ In Buffy's dream, she tells Tara that she needs to find the others. Be back in time for Dawn is the reply.

- Buffy abandons her mother to a life of living in the walls.

- She talks to Riley (who has just been made surgeon general) and a humanised Adam drawing up a plan for world domination.

- Finally, she finds herself in the desert with Tara and the first Slayer.

✒ And then, of course, there's the Cheese Guy. What the Hell is *that* all about?

MOMMY DEAREST:
The complicated psyche, lives and loves of Spike, the second vampire with a soul – Part 2

William the human was, frankly, a total mother's boy. His ailing mum was the true light of his life ('Lies My Parents Told Me'). She listened to his poetry and, bless her, professed to find it magnificent – seeming to share in William's fantasy world in which he was the heir to Byron, Shelley and Keats. Perhaps the first hint that William was to be no *ordinary* vampire came when, instead of emulating Angelus and massacring his family, William took his new paramour, Drusilla, home to meet mummy and proposed that the *three* of them embark on a career of slaughter and mayhem.

✍ One of William's first acts as a vampire was to sire his mother – and, thus, to give her the strength and energy that he himself had received. But, as a vampire, Anne was a very different character. She taunted her son concerning his stupidity and with the fact that his poetry was a load of sentimental twaddle. When she began to make disturbing sexual advances towards him, it was the final straw. William staked her, thus setting up a shed load of unresolved parental issues. Killing your mother once is worthy of a lifetime of therapy, but killing her *twice*? That's got to be some kind of record.

✍ Drusilla is, in a sense, Spike's surrogate mother as she actually made him what he is. But Spike always seems to crave

73

a little genuine and unconditional mother-love. He finds some in Joyce Summers.

The relationship between Spike and Joyce is one of the most touching in the series. It begins when Joyce, protecting her daughter, hits Spike on the head with an axe ('School Hard'). The two next meet when Buffy, introducing Spike to her mother as the lead singer in her new rock band (Buffy alleges that she is the drummer), invites him in for tea ('Becoming' Part 2). Spike and Joyce sit in an uneasy and formal silence on the couch.

Over the course of the next few years, Spike uses Joyce as a confidante. On his return to Sunnydale, he goes to Buffy's house for spell books and ends up companionably drinking hot chocolate and pouring out his grief at Drusilla's abandonment of him ('Lover's Walk'). Joyce is happy to have this personable young vampire in her kitchen and cheerfully hunts for the marshmallows he likes. When Angel arrives shortly afterwards, Joyce won't let *him* in the house, while Spike, amused, stands behind her making biting-style gestures.

Joyce and Dawn are forced to take refuge from Glory in Spike's crypt, and Joyce and Spike bond again over their shared love of the dreadful afternoon-TV soap-opera *Passions* ('Checkpoint'). Even when Spike discovers his love for Buffy and begins stalking her, Joyce thinks that Buffy must have led the poor boy on.

When Joyce dies, Spike is clearly as upset as everyone. Caught leaving an anonymous bunch of flowers for her funeral, he notes that Joyce treated him well and always had a cuppa and a kind word. Spike's subsequent help with Dawn's attempts to resurrect her mother seem, at least partly, for his own benefit ('Forever').

Spike is left motherless again and his burning issues remain unresolved until Robin Wood unwittingly assists him ('Lies My Parents Told Me'). When William sired his mother, he let loose a demon. His consequent burden of self-doubt and insecurity may explain why he killed so many other people's mothers (including, of course, Wood's). But Spike decides that his mother actually *did* love him. The demon within a vampire is informed by the human it once was (see 'Doppelgängland') but the explanation enables Spike to move on psychologically. Maybe, once Wood has sorted out his own problems, he has a future as a psychiatrist.

ADVANCED GEEK-SPEAK:
10 moments when *Buffy* characters betray their nerd credentials

This section details all of Warren, Jonathan and Andrew's media referencing, petty arguments about *Star Trek* and general *sadness*. And some of Xander's as well. Kindly remember this the next time you're at a *Buffy* convention and find yourself in a pointless discussion about whether Season 3 is better than Season 5. Which, by the way, it *is* … no, really, I've a chart and everything …

'Flooded': A whiteboard, in their lair, lists the *Troika*'s TO DO list. It's an ambitious conceit: CONTROL THE WEATHER, MINIATURIZE FORT KNOX, CONJURE FAKE IDS, SHRINK RAY, GIRLS and THE GORILLA THING. Jonathan also mentions a plan to create workable jet-packs – which they (sort of) eventually achieve – and adds HYPNOTIZE BUFFY at the end. Their references include:

- *The Wizard of Oz* (Andrew trained winged monkeys to attack the school play, which seems to have been a version of *Romeo and Juliet* judging by Jonathan's comments).

- *The Simpsons* and the *Austin Powers* movies (the *Troika*'s super-villain laugh being a straight cross between Dr Evil and Monty Burns).

- *Star Trek* (Jonathan and Andrew voting using the Vulcan hand gesture) and *Happy Days*.

- Andrew is upset because Warren won't build him a robot replica of *Sleepy Hollow* actress Christina Ricci.

🖉 'Life Serial': Warren and Jonathan find Andrew spray-painting a huge – and extremely conspicuous – mural of the Death Star on the side of their van. When Jonathan points out that one of the thermal exhaust ports is in the wrong place, Andrew proudly says that he's using the Empire's revised designs from *Return of the Jedi*.

- Andrew hopes that Buffy solves the time-loop that the *Troika* create for her faster than Data did on the episode of *Star Trek: The Next Generation* where the Enterprise kept blowing up ('Cause and Effect').

- Or, Warren adds, faster than Mulder in that *X-Files* episode where the bank kept exploding ('Monday').

- The pair allude to the Dead Parrot sketch from *Monty Python's Flying Circus*.

- When Andrew suggests that they're like Doctor No, a pointless argument ensues about who was the best James Bond.

- Warren admires Sean Connery, but Jonathan prefers the smooth Roger Moore. Andrew liked Timothy Dalton best.

- Warren's angry rant about the comedy aspects of *Moonraker* being inexcusable (the pigeon doing a double-take after the gondola sequence, for example), though representative of some of the louder – and more boring – voices in Bond fandom, is *way* off the mark. *Moonraker* is *funny*. And nowhere near as bad as *A View to a Kill*.

- One final point: Jonathan suggests that *The Living Daylights* (1986) was written for Roger Moore. Not, strictly speaking, true. Richard Maibaum and Michael Wilson's script was started during post-production on *A View to a Kill*, but it wasn't completed by the time that Moore left. Indeed, while most of the writing was going on, the actor that Eon Productions were trying to get to play the role was Pierce Brosnan, then starring in *Remington Steele*. Ordinarily this point would be far too anoraky to mention but, hell, this *is* the *Troika* we're talking about.

'Smashed': In the *Buffy* universe, seemingly, not only do all 703 episodes of the legendary British science-fiction TV series *Doctor Who* (1963–1996) still exist,[1] but they are also all available on DVD ... in Region 1, at least. The 80s comedy-SF show *Red Dwarf*, apparently, is not. Andrew descends from the ceiling of the museum à la Tom Cruise in *Mission Impossible*. Or, for that matter, like Frohike in the pilot episode of *The Lone Gunmen*.

'Gone': When Andrew sees Warren's Invisibility Ray he says that he had pictured something cooler. More ILM, less Ed Wood.

---

[1] In reality, over 100 of the 1960s monochrome *Doctor Who* episodes, from the William Hartnell and Patrick Troughton eras, are missing, presumed wiped, from the BBC's shamefully incomplete archives. Occasionally film prints of an odd episode turn up in some obscure third-world dictatorship or in the hand of a private collector (the most recent find of such a gem was in early 2004), but it's unlikely that we'll ever see television masterpieces like 'The Evil of the Daleks', 'Fury From the Deep' or 'The Web of Fear' in their entirety again.

- Industrial Light and Magic are a division of George Lucas's production company and are responsible for creating state-of-the-art special visual effects.

- Ed Wood was a director who made numerous notoriously cheap and camp movies, including the legendary *Plan 9 from Outer Space* – quite possibly the worst film ever made.

- Warren calls Jonathan Frodo in tribute to the vertically challenged hobbit from *The Lord of the Rings*.

 'Normal Again': There are references to:

- Douglas Adams's *The Hitch-Hikers Guide to the Galaxy*.

- The heist movie *Ocean's Eleven*.

- Jonathan mentions Jack Torrence, the hero of Stephen King's *The Shining* (as played with eye-rolling brilliance by Jack Nicholson in Stanley Kubrick's film adaptation).

- And the DC superhero comic *Legion of Doom*.

- Warren says that Andrew's demon has Buffy tripping like a Ken Russell film festival.

 'Grave': In a lengthy homage to the *Star Wars* movies, Andrew says that they have mere seconds before *Darth Rosenberg* grinds them all into Jawa-burgers and that not one of the Scooby Gang has the Midichlorians to stop her.

- Midichlorians are micro-organisms (*Star Wars Episode 1: The Phantom Menace*). Jedis have many Midichlorians, hence their psychic and supernatural abilities.

79

- Darth is the title given to a Sith Warrior (e.g. Darth Vader, Darth Maul).

- Jawas are the scavenger people who live on Tattooine.

- Other *Star Wars* references crop up in 'Dead Things' – Andrew and Jonathan sparring with plastic lightsabers; 'Entropy' – Warren calling Jonathan Padawan, the term for a trainee Jedi; and 'Never Leave Me' – Warren suggesting that his non-corporeality makes him like Obi-Wan Kenobi.

- Also, allusions to the *Uncanny X-Men* character Dark Phoenix (Jean Grey, formerly Marvel Girl, whose powers included telepathy and telekinesis; psychically seduced by the Hellfire Club, she was transformed into a power-hungry goddess and was, subsequently, killed).

- Andrew remembers that Superman's nemesis Lex Luthor had a false epidermis escape kit in *Superman versus the Amazing Spider-Man Treasury Edition*.

'Bring On the Night' witnesses a first sign of Xander's awkwardly re-emerging geek credentials: A guy knowing his Spider-Man, one can easily live with, but an encyclopaedic knowledge of *Wonder Woman* …? Get a life, dude, and *quickly*.

- In 'Doublemeat Palace', Xander shares the *Troika*'s taste in Vulcan sex objects, having a faraway look in his eyes when Willow mentions finding nude pictures of *Enterprise*'s Jolene Blalock. But that's a shade more understandable.

- When Andrew is told about The First, he notes that the entity's name isn't very ominous sounding. An evil name, he continues, should be like Lex Luthor or the Harry Potter novels' Voldemort.

- Andrew, subsequently, compares himself with the comic super-villains Dr Doom, Apocalypse and The Riddler. But now, he says, he has returned from the Dark Side, just as Darth Vadar did in the last five minutes of *Return of the Jedi*.

'Showtime': Andrew's description of how bored he is while tied to a chair involves a simile to *Star Wars Episode 1: The Phantom Menace*. Which is harsh but, probably, fair.

- Buffy asks Andrew if he ever saw the movie *Misery*. He replies that he did, six times. But he believes that Stephen King's novel was much scarier. Then he realises that Buffy is actually threatening him with something similar to what Kathy Bates did to James Caan in the movie and, quickly, he shuts up.

- There are also references to the Bond producers Albert and Barbara Broccoli, the movie *Licence To Kill* and its star, Timothy Dalton.

- And to the popular game Six Degrees of Kevin Bacon.

'Dirty Girls': Andrew, seemingly, believes that *Star Trek*'s Vulcans are real (confidently stating that it was, in fact, a blue-shirted Federation officer as opposed to a vulcanologist whom Faith murdered in 'Graduation Day' Part 1).

- When Amanda notes that Matthew Broderick killed Godzilla, Andrew and Xander are incandescent with rage. What Broderick killed, Xander notes, was actually a big dumb lizard that was *not* the real Godzilla in any way, shape or form. (Broderick was an actor whose earlier work Andrew told Jonathan he greatly admired in 'Two To Go'.)

Also referenced by the *Troika* in various episodes:

- *Indiana Jones and the Temple of Doom* (Warren calling Jonathan Short Round in 'Entropy').

- *Star Trek: The Next Generation* (Andrew describing Warren as Picard and Jonathan as Deanna Troi in 'Seeing Red').

- The *Back To The Future* movies ('Conversations With Dead People').

- Andrew notes that a nervous Jonathan has the same look on his face as he did that time Andrew highlighted in Jonathan's *Babylon 5* novels ('Entropy').

- The *Troika* have a (semi-naked) *Xena: Warrior Princess* action figure in their lair.

- When about to kill a piglet to open the Hellmouth Seal, Andrew observes that *Babe 2: Pig in the City* was a really underrated movie ('Never Leave Me').

- Andrew collects the classic Alan Moore comic *The League of Extraordinary Gentlemen* as, seemingly, does Xander ('The Killer in Me').

THE MAKING OF A MONSTER:
The complicated psyche, lives and loves of Spike,
the second vampire with a soul – Part 3

✍ Once Spike became a vampire he was through with society's rules. He needed a new image. First to go were the cultured tones of the gentleman. William quickly adopted the rough speech and dress of the working classes, affecting a harsh cockney accent much to the annoyance of the more aristocratic Angelus.

✍ For Spike, image is everything. His style and his manner of speech are calculated to scream *rebel*. Over the course of his undead life Spike has had many moments of despair, but it's significant that the sole occasion on which we see him suicidal ('Doomed') is because his jeans have shrunk in the wash and he's been forced to borrow Xander's nerdish clothes.

✍ William also got in touch with his violent side, developing a penchant for brawling. This, together with his habit of torturing his victims with railroad spikes, attracted the attention of several angry mobs, forcing Angelus's crew to flee the capital to the relative safety of Yorkshire ('Fool for Love'). (It's tempting to hope that the taunting toff from Cecily's party who would rather have a spike driven through his head than listen to any more of William's poetry did, indeed, get his wish.)

✍ William adopts a new name and, at the same time, develops an obsession with the mythology of the Slayer.

Unlike Angelus, Spike is keen to seek out and kill these mythical teenage warriors. His first encounter, during the Chinese Boxer rebellion, gave him his trademark eyebrow scar. (And a mystery. Why the scar? Vampires have accelerated healing powers. If Spike scars he should look like a patchwork quilt by now. Maybe he wanted to keep that one for aesthetic reasons, as part of the growing legend of Spike – the vampire who kills Slayers.)

Spike claims to have been at Woodstock in 1969 (presumably he had a tent during the daytime). Perhaps thankfully, no photos of Hippy Spike have yet appeared. (A flashback in the *Angel* episode 'The Girl in Question' shows a very beatnik-influenced Spike and Dru in Rome in the 1950s.) It wasn't until the emergence of punk in London in 1976 that Spike finally found his look (one, he subsequently told Buffy, that was stolen from him by a young Bromley art student called Billy Idol).

He retained his peroxide hair, although he soon ditched the eyeliner and studded belt. His most iconic accessory was a leather coat stripped from the back of Slayer Nikki Wood after he killed her on a New York subway train in 1977. It's still wearing well over two decades later.

So, piece by piece, the monster was created: the name, the accent, the scar, the coat, the hair, the arrogance. Yet it's all stripped away in moments when, for the second time in his life, a woman's rejection of him leaves him sobbing in an alley. In 120 years of careful image-building, he's come precisely nowhere. He's still the same insecure guy and all it takes to break him are three words: 'You're beneath me' ('Fool for Love').

'THE PLAY'S THE THING …'

Classic theatrical and literature references or allusions in *Buffy* include:

- Elizabeth Barrett Browning's *Sonnets from the Portuguese* ('The Witch', 'Helpless', 'Two To Go')

- *Macbeth* ('I, Robot … You, Jane', 'The Wish', 'Tabula Rasa')

- *Oedipus Rex* ('The Puppet Show')

- *The Merchant of Venice* ('Out of Mind, Out of Sight')

- *Hamlet* ('Prophecy Girl', 'The Dark Age', 'Lies My Parents Told Me')

- Kate Douglas Wiggin's *Rebecca of Sunnybrooke Farm* ('What's My Line?' Part 2)

- *Henry IV, Part 1* ('Surprise')

- Greek poet Homer ('Killed By Death')

- *Julius Caesar* ('I Only Have Eyes For You', 'Fear Itself', 'Conversations With Dead People')

- Arthur Miller's *Death of a Salesman* ('Band Candy', 'Restless')

- Jean-Paul Sartre's *La Nausée* ('Lover's Walk')

- PG Wodehouse ('The Wish')

- Aldous Huxley's *Brave New World* ('The Wish')

- Samuel Beckett's *Waiting for Godot* ('Enemies')

- *Othello* ('Earshot')

- Jack Kerouac's *On the Road* ('Choices')

- Robert Frost's 'Stopping By Woods On A Snowy Evening' ('The Prom', 'Graduation Day' Part 2)

- Another Frost poem, 'The Death of the Hired Man' ('Pangs').

- W Somerset Maugham's *Of Human Bondage* ('The Freshman')

- Tom Wolfe's *The Electric Kool-Aid Acid Test* ('Beer Bad')

- Stevie Smith's 'Not Waving but Drowning' ('Something Blue', 'All the Way')

- WB Yates's 'The Second Coming' ('Doomed', 'Entropy')

- William Burroughs ('New Moon Rising')

- Greek poet Sappho ('Restless')

- Samuel Taylor Coleridge's *The Rime of the Ancient Mariner* ('The Replacement')

- Sir Walter Scott's *Marmion* ('Family')

- Anton Chekhov ('Into the Woods')

- Dr Seuss's *The Cat in the Hat* ('Triangle')

- Frances Hodgson's *The Little Princess* ('Tough Love')

- *Henry V* ('The Gift', 'All the Way', 'Hell's Bells')

- Henry David Thoreau's *Walden, or Life in the Woods* ('Bargaining' Part 1)

- *Moby Dick* ('All the Way')

- *As You Like It* ('Once More, With Feeling')

- William Cowper's *The Timepiece* ('Doublemeat Palace') and *Olney Hymns* ('Dirty Girls')

- Dostoyevski's *Crime and Punishment* ('Villains')

- *King Lear* ('Same Time, Same Place', 'Dirty Girls')

- Kurt Vonnegut's *Slaughterhouse Five* ('Help')

- Louisa May Alcott's *Little Women* ('Touched')

'I'M BUFFY THE VAMPIRE SLAYER. AND YOU ARE ...?':

12 great lines of dialogue from *Buffy*'s Season 3

Giles's sarcastic impression of Joyce: '"Do you like my mask? Isn't it pretty? It raises the dead!" *Americans*!' – 'Dead Man's Party'

Xander's reaction to Faith's semi-erotic Slaying tale: 'Wow, they should film *that* and show it every Christmas.' – 'Faith, Hope and Trick'

The teenage-like Giles on Buffy's limp interrogation technique: 'You're *my* Slayer. Go knock his teeth down his throat.' – 'Band Candy'

Spike, on Buffy and Angel as a couple: 'Love isn't brains, children, it's blood ... I may be love's bitch, but at least I'm man enough to admit it.' – 'Lover's Walk'

Cordelia, on the world she left behind: 'Buffy changes it. It was better, I mean the clothes alone. The people were happy. Mostly.' – 'The Wish'

Buffy: 'I'm like ... the boy that stuck his finger in the duck.' Angel: 'Dyke. It's another word for dam.' Buffy: 'OK, that story makes a lot more sense now.' – 'Gingerbread'

Xander, on his new car: 'It's my thing.' Buffy: 'Is this a penis metaphor?' – 'The Zeppo'

Buffy, to the replacement Watcher, Wesley: 'Whenever Giles sends me on a mission, he always says "Please". And afterwards, I get a cookie.' – 'Bad Girls'

A bewildered Willow as Buffy and Xander, realising that she's not a vampire, hug her: 'Oxygen becoming an issue.' – 'Doppelgängland'

Cordelia, trying to discover if Mr Beech is a would-be murderer: 'I was just wondering, were you planning on killing a bunch of people tomorrow? It's for the yearbook.' – 'Earshot'

Anya's brutal honesty surfaces for the first time: 'I've seen some horrible things in my time. I've been the cause of most of them, actually.' – 'Graduation Day' Part 1

Mayor Wilkins, to one of his vampire minions: 'We don't *knock* during dark rituals?' – 'Graduation Day' Part 1

'IF YOU'VE GOTTA GO …':

20 outrageously inventive deaths of characters in *Buffy*

Principal Bob Flutie: Eaten by several hyena-possessed and, presumably, hungry students ('The Pack').

Nurse Greenliegh: Fed to the steroid-altered Sunnydale High swim team by Coach Marin ('Go Fish').

Coach Marin: Probably sexually assaulted and, certainly, eaten by the same swim team. *That'll* teach him ('Go Fish').

Joyce's extremely annoying neighbour, Pat: Possessed by the spirit of an African tribal mask, then had a garden spade driven though her eyes ('Dead Man's Party').

Doctor Gregory: Eaten by a giant She-Mantis ('Teacher's Pet').

Zachary Kralic: Tricked into drinking holy water with fatal consequences ('Helpless').

Rodney Munson: Desiccated by a recently revived South American princess ('Inca Mummy Girl').

Gwendolyn Post: Arm sliced off with a jagged shard of glass and the rest of her body consumed by mystical lightning ('Revelations').

Principal Snyder: Head bitten off by the Mayor of Sunnydale ('Graduation Day' Part 2).

Mayor Richard Wilkins III: Blown to smithereens inside an exploding school and toasted extra crispy ('Graduation Day' Part 2).

Professor Gerhardt: Stabbed by a Chumash warrior spirit with an ancient ritual knife ('Pangs').

Jack O'Toole: Shot. Then raised from the dead by his grandpappy's mojo. Then ripped apart by an enraged were-wolf in the school boiler room ('The Zeppo').

Balthazar: Electrocuted in a very big bathtub ('Bad Girls').

Gachnar, the fear demon: Stamped upon by Buffy's stylish yet affordable boot ('Fear Itself').

Scabby demon: Squashed by a collapsing skyjack ('Life Serial').

Warren Meers: Flayed alive by a very pissed-off Wicca ('Villains').

Philip Henry: Decomposed into mercurial goo ('The Dark Ages').

Ken: Victim of the world's first *totally lethal* Mahatma Gandhi impersonation ('Anne').

The Last of The Seven: Stabbed in the back by a ventrilo-quist's dummy. Then decapitated by a magician's trick guillotine as a prelude to the school talent contest ('The Puppet Show').

Caleb: Emasculated and bifurcated (in one movement) with a mystical axe ('Chosen').

SID AND NANCY:

The complicated psyche, lives and loves of Spike,
the second vampire with a soul – Part 4

Beautiful, vicious, fey, *mad as toast* – Drusilla was Spike's
love for over a hundred years. She saw William's potential,
almost certainly relieved him of his virginity and tutored him
in the ways of evil. Spike still keeps a spare set of chains
around, just in case she ever comes back ('The Harsh Light of
Day'). Dru even appreciated his poetry ('Crush') (on this
point, of course, it's important to remember that the girl is
completely insane).

Interrupted by Drusilla in the midst of his vainglorious
introduction of himself to The Anointed One in 'School
Hard', Spike instantly drops the bravado and tenderly wraps
his fragile beloved in his coat. It's immediately evident that
these are no ordinary vampires.

In 'Surprise', when he's with Dru, Spike drops his Big
Bad persona to reveal a tender and caring side. He seems desperate not to upset her, is fiercely protective and abjectly
apologetic for his momentary loss of temper. Dru, in her
weakened state, is a liability, but her visions and prescient
dreams are, occasionally, useful. The only aspect of their relationship that bothers him is her shared past with Angelus.
Spike is unhappy even to allow Dru to torture Angel and
becomes a seething mass of jealousy when his sire and grand
sire meet ('Lie To Me').

Dru almost died at the hands of a mob in Prague and Spike brought her to the Hellmouth to seek a cure. It's lucky that Dru's sire, Angel, is in town because the Ritual of Du Lac is (literally) what the doctor ordered. Sunnydale also contains plenty of ruined churches and, indeed, the Cross of Du Lac. But first there's time for a takeover bid, an attempt to kill the Slayer and the assassination of The Anointed One ('School Hard').

Angel is saved and Spike is badly injured ('What's My Line?' Part 2). Dru, restored by the partly completed ritual, becomes Spike's carer. But Spike still commands enough minions to secure The Judge as a novel birthday gift for Dru ('Surprise'). Angelus's subsequent taunting of Spike and his resumption of a relationship with Dru drive Spike to despair and impotent rage ('Innocence'). Desperate to win back Dru and preserve the future of dog racing, Manchester United and Happy Meals on Legs, a restored Spike enters into a secret pact with Buffy ('Becoming' Part 1).

Spike and Dru have travelled the world and happily reminisce about their adventures in France, Vienna and Spain ('Surprise'). Later journeys will take them to South America, where Dru embarks on a brief but torrid affair with a chaos demon, a personable creature despite his slime-and-antlers appearance. The breakdown of Spike and Dru's relationship leaves him a heartbroken, drunken wreck ('Lover's Walk').

Dru is next in Sunnydale when she's trying to bring her boy back to the fold, taking him dancing at The Bronze. But her problem is not so much the electrical impulses controlling Spike, rather it's his obsession with Buffy ('Crush').

A lovelorn Spike notes that he considered himself lucky just to have touched such a black beauty. But, to prove his love for Buffy, he will gladly stake Drusilla. Dru may be insane but even she isn't going to stick around for long after that. So Spike and Dru's 120-year-old love affair ends. Spike's plan doesn't go down too well with Buffy or Harmony either and Spike manages to lose all the three women in his life in one go. Even for Spike, that's quite a feat.

WE HARDLY KNEW YE, BUT WE KILLED YE ANYWAY:
10 further outrageously inventive deaths of extras in *Buffy*

Vampire: Decapitated in The Bronze with a flying cymbal ('The Harvest').

Police Officer: Face gruesomely ripped off by a Gavrox demon ('Choices').

Fat Vampire: Assassinated with the aid of a cigarette lighter ('Bargaining' Part 1).

Vampire: Head removed by a slamming car door ('All the Way').

Vampire: Head hacked off with an autopsy saw ('The Body').

Man in a Suit: Forced to dance himself into self-immolation ('Once More, With Feeling').

Hooker in Alley: Used as a human cigarette filter by Angelus ('Innocence').

Student: Heart removed (without the benefit of either local or general anaesthetic) by a Gentleman ('Hush').

Student: Head exploded due to excessive stress ('Storyteller').

 Vampire: Staked with a – presumably quite sharp – pool cue ('Doppelgängland').

CANCEL MY SUBSCRIPTION TO THE RESURRECTION:

15 Sunnydale inhabitants who make the greatest comeback since Lazarus and simply refuse to *stay* dead

🗡 Mr Sanderson from the bank ('Gingerbread'). Returned as a vampire. Killed by Buffy.

🗡 Xander's friend-dude Jesse ('The Harvest'). Returned as a vampire. Killed, accidentally, by Xander.

🗡 Football star Daryl Epps ('Some Assembly Required'). Brought back to life, Frankenstein-like, by his brother Chris and his friend Eric.

🗡 Buffy's classmate Theresa Klusmeyer ('Phases'). Returned as a vampire (having been sired by Angelus). Killed by Buffy.

🗡 Ghostly star-crossed lovers Grace Newman and James Stanley ('I Only Have Eyes For You'). Remained haunting the school due to the tragedy of their deaths until freed by Buffy and Angelus.

🗡 Various members of the Sunnydale High swim team, including Cameron Walker, Gage Petronzi and Dodd McAlvy ('Go Fish'). Became aquatic monsters.

Cordelia's best friend, Harmony Kendall. Bitten by a vampire ('Graduation Day' Part 2). Next seen as a vampire ('The Harsh Light of Day' and numerous episodes afterwards). Currently a personal assistant in the Los Angeles branch of law firm Wolfram & Hart.

Psychotic Jack O'Toole and his jock friends Bob, Parker and Dickie ('The Zeppo'). Raised by the remarkably unspecific results of Jack's grandfather's mojo.

Sandy. Sired by Evil Willow ('Doppelgängland'). Later got rather friendly with Riley ('Family', 'Shadow'), who subsequently killed her.

Buffy's student friend Eddie ('The Freshman'). Returned as a vampire. Killed by Buffy.

Professor Maggie Walsh, Doctor Angleman and Forrest Gates (died, respectively, in 'The I in Team', 'Goodbye Iowa' and 'The Yoko Factor'). Reanimated by Adam as mindless drones ('Primeval').

The various manifest spirits controlled by a talisman in the Sunnydale High basement ('Lessons').

Psychology student Holden Webster ('Conversations With Dead People'). Returned as a vampire. Killed by Buffy.

Glory's minion Doc ('The Weight of the World'). Killed by Buffy.

Buffy Summers, Vampire Slayer ('Prophecy Girl', 'The Gift'). She saved the world. A lot.

WORK IS A FOUR-LETTER WORD:
Some less-than-successful career opportunities in *Buffy*

For the first three years of *Buffy*'s existence, it was all so uncomplicated in matters related to work. Most of the characters were in high school and their only work-related fears were ending up sweeping the floor at the pizza place and asking the kids where the cool parties are this weekend ('The Pack'). Giles, as representative of the adult workforce, was an example of that rarest of things: someone who had an occupation they actually *like*. Joyce, similarly, was a self-employed art-gallery owner, though it meant that, on more than one occasion, she seemed more interested in this than in her daughter. Nevertheless, with a departure from school, for several of the characters the real game of life was just beginning.

The Harris family have something of a history of dead-end jobs. There are several allusions to Xander's father being frequently unemployed (notably in 'Bad Girls' and 'Hell's Bells').

- Xander's uncle worked at the local Computer Research & Development plant – in a floor-sweeping capacity, admittedly ('I, Robot ... You, Jane').

- The family's self-employed taxidermist, Uncle Rory, eventually lost his business, due in no small part to his heavy drinking and whoring ('The Dark Age', 'The Zeppo', 'Hell's Bells').

So, when Xander entered the employment field, unsurprisingly it was *not* as a trainee brain surgeon. Returning to Sunnydale after his post-graduation sabbatical, Xander revealed that he had spent the summer working in the kitchen (and, it is heavily implied, on the stage) of Oxnard's Fabulous Ladies Strip Club ('The Freshman'). Later, Xander became the new barman at the UC Sunnydale college pub. Needless to say, he was hopeless at it ('Beer Bad').

Other somewhat unwise career moves that Xander subsequently had a go at included:

- Working at the local Hot Dog on a Stick emporium (alluded to in 'Pangs').

- A pizza-delivery boy ('Doomed').

- Selling Boost energy bars ('The I in Team').

- Driving an ice-cream van ('Where the Wild Things Are', 'Restless').

- Working at a Starbucks coffee house and on a telephone sex line (both mentioned in 'The Yoko Factor' as jobs he was fired from).

By 'Primeval' he's so depressed he can hardly be bothered to get out of bed and go to the employment office.

Finally, in the field of construction, Xander found something that he was actually quite good at – although his career as a digger and manual labourer got off to an inauspicious start after a few days on the sick with mystical syphilis ('Pangs').

- Again, family history suggested an affinity with construction work – Xander mentions that his Uncle Dave was a plumber ('I Was Made to Love You').

- By the time of 'The Replacement' Xander has been working for a construction firm, as a carpenter, for three months. And, despite Uncool Xander's reservations about his own abilities, the foreman asks Cool Xander to head the Interior Carpentry crew on a new job in Carlton.

- From there, this glorified bricklayer (according to a jealous Spike in 'The Gift') enters management level. But for the little complication of his entire town disappearing into a hole in the ground ('Chosen'), here's one ex-Sunnydale High *alumni* made good.

When he loses his job as the librarian of the now-blown-up Sunnydale High, Giles enters a period of unemployment and readjustment. This involves:

- Renewing relationships with old acquaintances ('The Freshman').

- Watching lots of daytime TV ('The Harsh Light of Day').

Finally pulling himself out of his depression, Giles notes the financial rewards of The Magic Box shop and, despite the establishment's previous proprietors having the life expectancy of a Spinal Tap drummer, he realises that any owner who manages to survive frequent vampire attacks is sitting on a potential gold mine ('Real Me').

Anya reveals a natural talent for shop work (and capitalist greed) and subsequently becomes Giles's assistant at The Magic

Box ('No Place Like Home'). She has such a flair for it that she eventually becomes Giles's partner ('Bargaining') and, when he returns to England ('Tabula Rasa'), the sole proprietor.

When Buffy's financial troubles manifest themselves ('Flooded'), she decides to drop out of college and find work. Xander gets Buffy a labouring job on his building site ('Life Serial'). Her strength is an advantage in overcoming the sexism of the crew, but she's actually *too good* at it. As they get paid by the hour she is told to slow down. Andrew's demons finally put an end to Buffy's construction career.

Buffy reluctantly tries the retail trade, working for Giles and Anya at The Magic Box ... with hilarious consequences ('Life Serial').

The Doublemeat Palace is one of California's biggest fast-food chains. Their speciality, the Doublemeat Medley, includes a closely guarded secret ingredient, which, Buffy speculates due to circumstantial evidence, is actually *people*. It isn't, as she subsequently discovers when working there; rather, it's a blend of vegetable products. The company, nevertheless, are keen that their customers don't discover that they are actually eating veggie burgers. Buffy, having been sacked for her outburst in the restaurant, gets her job back by promising to keep the secret a secret. However, drawbacks include:

- The fact that she leaves work with a smell that lingers for hours and the mind-numbing nature of the work ('Dead Things').

- The long hours ('Older and Far Away').

- Wearing a cow on her hat ('As You Were').

Buffy eventually quits to work at the recently reopened Sunnydale High. Robin Wood offers her an, admittedly low-paid, part-time counselling job with the school's Outreach programme, aimed at helping troubled teenagers ('Lessons').

SLAYER

THE BOY LOOKED AT JOHNNY:
10 defining Jonathan Levinson moments in *Buffy*

Of all the journey's made by semi-regular characters in *Buffy*, that of Jonathan Levinson is one of the most conceptually satisfying. Initially little more than a walk-on who got a couple of lines, Jonathan became – via Danny Strong's wonderfully innocent-faced delivery – one of the series' most loved characters.

Introduced in 'Inca Mummy Girl', Jonathan is the student who narrowly avoids having the life sucked out of him by Ampata before Xander intervenes. Poor guy, it was probably the first time in his life that a beautiful woman had ever hit on him, and she turns out to be an evil corpse.

In 'Reptile Boy', dressed in his best suit, Jonathan is in The Bronze on what appears to be a date with Cordelia (at least, he's fetching her a cinnamon and chocolate, half-caf, non-fat coffee ... and forgetting the extra foam).

- It's true that Harmony and the other Cordettes use Jonathan as the punchline of a cruel joke at Cordelia's expense after she's broken up with Xander ('The Wish').

- Despite this, there seems to be a genuine affinity between the shy little fat kid and the bitchy prom queen.

- In 'Homecoming' Cordelia considers Jonathan important enough to bribe him to vote for her in the Homecoming Queen elections.

- In the aftermath of the Mayor's ascension, it's Jonathan who comforts a clearly upset Cordy ('Graduation Day' Part 2).

✍ During the Sunnydale High Career Day, police officer Patrice – in reality, the third member of the Order of Taraka assassins sent to kill Buffy – grabs Jonathan as a hostage. Chased out of the building by Kendra, Buffy and Willow are slightly more concerned with the shot Oz than with a confused Jonathan, who merely asks if that was all a demonstration.

✍ There's a wonderfully deadpan humour involved in several early Jonathan appearances:

- He arrives at the school library to get a biography on Stalin in 'Passion' to find a Scooby Gang meeting in full swing and Xander asking, angrily, if he hasn't heard of knocking.

- In 'Dead Man's Party' he's invited by Buffy to join in a furious argument developing between the Slayer and her friends.

- In 'Go Fish', having twice tried out for the school swim team, and failing to obtain a place, Jonathan is bullied by Dodd and Cameron during the team's victory beach party. When both subsequently appear to die, Willow suspects Jonathan and interrogates him, suggesting that he conjured up a Hellbeast from the ocean's depths as revenge. No, replies Jonathan, actually he peed in the pool.

✌ Having gained the power of telepathy ('Earshot'), Buffy learns that someone on campus is planning to kill all the students. She finds Jonathan alone in the school's clock tower with a rifle. Buffy gets Jonathan to give her the weapon, only to realise that he was intending to kill himself and not everyone else.

✌ Touchingly, a sequel to this drama is played out in 'The Prom':

• Jonathan is asked to give Buffy a special award from her fellow students.

• 'We're not good friends,' Jonathan notes. 'Most of us never found the time to get to know you.' But that doesn't mean that they haven't noticed Buffy.

• They don't talk about it much, but it's no secret that Sunnydale High isn't like other high schools.

• But, whenever something creepy has happened, Buffy always seemed to be there to stop it.

• They are proud, therefore, to note that the Class of 99 has the lowest mortality rate in Sunnydale High's history.

• They also know, to a large extent, that it's because of Buffy Summers, Class Protector.

✌ Suave, cool, super-successful – Jonathan Levinson is *everyone's* hero, living in his Sunnydale mansion with gorgeous blonde Swedish twins. Among other things, he's a movie star, a singer, a basketball player and a better fighter than Buffy the Vampire Slayer, who takes orders from and looks up to him. However, Buffy begins to suspect that Jonathan's a little *too* perfect:

- How, for instance, did he star in *The Matrix* without ever leaving Sunnydale?

- How did he finish medical school by the age of eighteen?

- What's the deal with the mysterious scar on his upper arm?

- Jonathan's behaviour regarding a new monster in town is also suspicious.

Buffy concludes that Jonathan has altered the world to change how people perceive him, and the Scooby Gang's research, much to their disappointment, supports this theory. Jonathan admits to performing an augmentation spell, which created the evil monster currently terrorising Sunnydale. With Buffy's help, Jonathan destroys the monster and returns everything to reality ('Superstar').

Having joined up with fellow Nerds of Doom, Warren Meers and Andrew Wells ('Flooded'), Jonathan and his buddies decide to become evil arch fiends and take over Sunnydale, starting with a convoluted test of the Slayer's perception ('Life Serial'). The *Troika*'s subsequent plans include:

- Creating an invisibility weapon ('Gone').

- A freeze-ray devised as part of a plan to steal a diamond ('Smashed').

Warren's sick plan of creating a cerebral dampener to make women their sex slaves, however, has predictable consequences

('Dead Things') and leads to a schism between them. Jonathan and Andrew are eventually captured by Buffy when a jet-pack escape goes disastrously wrong ('Seeing Red').

- Following Tara's murder, Jonathan and Andrew evade the wrath of a vengeful Willow ('Two To Go', 'Grave') and flee to Mexico ('Storyteller').

- They return to Sunnydale, ostensibly to help the Slayer and gain redemption.

- In reality, Jonathan has been betrayed and he is murdered by Andrew to open the Seal of Danzalthar, which covers the Hellmouth ('Conversations With Dead People').

SOUL2SOUL:
The complicated psyche, lives and loves of Spike, the second vampire with a soul – Part 5

So, what's the deal with Spike telling Angel 'You were my sire, man'? ('School Hard'). One could, perhaps, understand why the idiots at The Council of Watchers might get something as important as who was responsible for William The Bloody existing so spectacularly wrong (Spike's age, misquoted in *The Watcher's Diaries*, is a case in point). But surely Spike himself knows his own father? The official explanation is that your sire is not necessarily the vampire that made you – rather, it's a family thing.

It's like one of those early chapters in the Bible: The Master begat Darla. Darla begat Angelus. Angelus begat Drusilla. Dru begat Spike. All these generations of vampires belong to the Order of Aurelius, though, after a falling-out between The Master and Angelus during the 1760s, their links to the Order are tenuous at best these days.

When Dru sired Spike, the young William The Bloody was a bit of a liability with his penchant for inciting mob violence ('Fool for Love'). It is, thus, not unreasonable to assume that Angelus undertook to teach the lad a thing or two about life as vampire.

Angelus's *modus-operandi* is all about exquisite mental cruelty and the artistry of the kill. His pupil, by contrast, champions brawling and the persuasive ways of a railroad spike. Spike thinks that, frankly, Angelus is a *poofter*. Angelus believes that Spike is an idiot. Yet neither stakes the other and they trade insults like a demonic comedy double-act – grudging respect mingled with bitter rivalry.

The fanged Gang of Four (Angelus, Darla, Drusilla and Spike) had just eighteen years to wreak glorious havoc across the capital cities of Europe before, in 1898, Darla's gift to Angelus of a gypsy girl led to him being cursed with a soul ... and becoming, in Darla's eyes, the filthy and disgusting Angel ('Becoming' Part 1). It is unclear how much of this Spike and Dru are privy to. Certainly, when Angel returns briefly to their family, during The Boxer Rebellion two years later ('Fool for Love'), Spike takes Angel's offhand reaction to his killing the Slayer as caustic jealousy when, in reality, it is revulsion.

When Giles seeks information about the new vampire on the block, Angel accords Spike due respect – he notes that he is worse than anything the Slayer has faced before. Angelus's protégé has become a legendary killer of Slayers and, while he's in town, he intends to add another to his tally. Once he starts something, Angel adds, Spike won't stop until everything in his path is dead ('School Hard'). It's almost as if Angel feels a perverse sort of pride in Spike's notorious exploits.

It's been an age since the squabbling siblings last met and Spike is overjoyed to see his mentor, greeting him with an enthusiastic hug. Angel, posing as Angelus, offers to share a Xander-flavoured snack while explaining that his *tortured and brooding* act keeps the not-too-bright current Slayer off his back. Luckily for Xander, Spike sees through Angel's disguise and reacts with disgust.

🖋 He and Angel tangle in Sunnydale on several occasions and, though Xander doesn't seem to have taken his curiosity about the term 'sire' to the Scooby's research meetings, Angel confesses to Buffy that he sired Dru having first driven her insane. Of all the unconscionable things that Angel did in his life, Dru, he considers, was by far the worst. Spike obviously holds a different view. However, Spike is uneasy about Drusilla and Angelus's shared history. When Angel is captured by Spike for the ritual of Du Lac ('What's My Line?' Part 2), Spike is clearly a mass of seething insecurity.

🖋 Spike's subsequent period of confinement to a wheelchair means the Big Bad is now helpless and dependent on his girl-friend. But there's one bright spot on the horizon: the return of Angelus who, after a spot of post-traumatic lovemaking with Buffy, is now *sans* soul. The baddest vamp in all the land is back in business and Spike seems overjoyed at this develop-ment. He welcomes rather less, however, Angelus's immediate assumption of Spike's role as *paterfamilias* and the inevitable rekindling of their endless slanging matches and Angelus taunting Spike over his disabilities. Drusilla is delighted to have her boys back together and fighting over her, and she plays the situation for all it's worth. Spike is even less pleased when Angel's rash behaviour and his targeting of Buffy's immediate family and friends – culminating in the murder of Jenny Calendar ('Passion') – leads to the arrival at their hide-out of one very pissed-off Watcher.

🖋 Angel moves his family into the Crawford Street mansion and continues to infuriate Spike by emphasising the apparent rekindling of his sexual relationship with Drusilla. Maddened with betrayal, and having secretly regained his former strength and mobility, the cuckolded lover forms an unlikely alliance with the Slayer, double crossing Angelus by using his knowledge of Dru's powers of hypnosis to save Giles's life. Spike drives off with an unconscious Drusilla – for which Drusilla will never forgive him.

Angel ultimately returns from Hell and attempts to pursue a platonic friendship with Buffy. It takes a drunken Spike to explain, eloquently, why this will never work. He has a remarkable degree of insight into the doomed dynamics of a Slayer/Vampire relationship. This will come in handy later, but for now Spike roars out of town again, 'My Way' blasting on his stereo, with the sole intention of finding Drusilla, tying her up and torturing her until she loves him again. He leaves Angel and Buffy to, ultimately, end their affair ('Lover's Walk').

For all his confident swagger, Spike will always carry around unresolved issues with his grand sire. While in the throes of a magically induced engagement with Buffy ('Something Blue'), he falls into petulant jealousy when his fiancée mentions her ex-lover, and even takes the trouble to have his Buffy robot programmed with various anti-Angel put-downs ('Intervention').

Finally, Spike wins himself a soul and, unlike Angel, Spike's has no inconvenient happiness curse attached to it. However, he will not tolerate any comparisons with his grand sire. He is, he insists to Faith, *nothing* like Angel, who's as dull as a table lamp and has *very* different colouring ('Dirty Girls'). When Angel learns that Spike not only has a soul but also is involved with the Slayer, he is appalled ('Chosen'). Getting the brush-off in favour of Captain Peroxide was not part of the plan. Having watched Buffy and Angel's tender reunion, Spike beats his punchbag adorned with a childlike cartoon vampire whose hair grows straight up. Sadly, we never see Buffy's suggested solution of putting the two ensouled vampires in a locked room and letting them wrestle it out ... perhaps with oil of some kind being involved.

Spike, meanwhile, takes his sire's place as champion and, fuelled by the power of his soul and the magical amulet that Angel brought from Los Angeles to Sunnydale, finally moves out of Angel's shadow by saving the world and earning his redemption at the cost of his own life.

SLAYER

LOGIC, LET ME INTRODUCE YOU TO THIS WINDOW:
10 things in *Buffy the Vampire Slayer* that make absolutely no logical sense whatsoever

It is *inevitable* that, even in the most inventive and intelligent of series, there are going to be a few goofs, plot-holes, logic mistakes and continuity errors. Part of the fun of being a fan is looking for these and pointing them out, loudly, on the Internet. Then, when any non-fans point out the same things, hitting them hard on the top of the head with this book. Here are some of the more thought-provoking screw-ups in *Buffy*.

How can vampires, who it's well established cast no reflection, be photographed or filmed when both cameras and camcorders use mirrors as part of their focusing mechanism?

If one vampire is capable of redemption ('Grave') and a spell for re-ensouling vampires also exists ('Becoming' Part 2), then shouldn't Buffy be trying to re-ensoul and redeem vampires rather than merely slaying them? It's a longer process, admittedly, but it's surely a more humane one. Or does this only work on vampires that she fancies?

Why do a vampire's clothes turn to dust when they do, even if they are not necessarily the clothes that the vampire was buried in? It's worth noting that other objects worn by vampires (rings, for example – see 'Never Kill a Boy on the First Date', 'Surprise') seem *not* to be affected by this phenomena.

 Willow asks something that many of us have been dying to know the answer to. If they cast no reflection, how do vampires shave? ('Reptile Boy').

 How do male vampires have sex? ('Surprise', 'Wrecked') Biologically speaking, it takes a great deal of increased blood circulation for a man to achieve an erection. Unless, of course, they've had one since they were sired. If that's the case, then it must, frankly, be rather tiresome for the vampire concerned.

Other things that vampires can do that you probably didn't know corpses could include:

- The ability to breathe ('Innocence')

- Bleed ('Graduation Day' Part 1)

- Eat food ('Hush').

 And why is the amount of blood taken by a vampire given such focus in 'Helpless' – Kralik mentions it twice in relation to firstly Blair and then Buffy – and then never mentioned anywhere else within the series?

 What is Angel's source of income when he's living in Sunnydale? If he didn't have one – as seems likely – then how did he pay his phone bills and rent?

 Some of the paramedics' actions in 'The Body' are inaccurate:

- They shouldn't have called the time of death (in most states, including California, only a doctor can do that).

115

- Joyce should have been taken to hospital where she would have been declared Dead On Arrival.

- Once attempts at resuscitation had been started by paramedics, they should not have been stopped until the patient was transferred to someone with a higher degree of medical training, and certainly not for the reason that the paramedics had another call to go to.

- Chest compressions should be done with straight arms, at a 90° angle to the ground, slower than depicted by either Buffy or the medic and much deeper. For Buffy, this was to be expected but, for trained medical staff, it was inexcusable. (Doing chest compressions *properly* on an actor is probably not going to be good for their health.)

- It's unlikely (though not inconceivable) that Buffy would have been left alone with the body. The police should also have been called to conduct a preliminary interview and determine cause of death.

The timescale of much of Season 7 is wildly illogical. 'Conversations With Dead People' began on 12 November and concluded in the early hours of the next morning. 'Sleeper' followed directly from that episode, covering approximately two days. 'Never Leave Me' followed directly from *that* with a similar timescale and 'Showtime' did likewise – note that in all cases the cast were wearing the same clothes at the beginning of each episode as they were at the end of the previous one. The events of 'Showtime' should, therefore, be dated no later than 18 or 19 November. Yet it's stated within the episode's dialogue that it's now December, shortly before Christmas.

It is never fully resolved what, specifically, Buffy did to allow The First the opportunity to raise the vampire army and open the Hellmouth:

- The implication is that it was something to do with Buffy having returned from the afterlife in 'Bargaining' Part 1, which was certainly a unique situation. (In the *Angel* episode 'Inside Out', Skip alludes to the uniqueness of this when he tells Angel that no one has ever returned from paradise. Except for a Slayer, once.)

- However, it is equally possible that events such as Buffy sending Angel to Hell ('Becoming' Part 2) – something that The Powers That Be specifically had to intervene in to correct – or Buffy sleeping with Angel ('Surprise'), which directly led to the latter event, could have caused the kinds of cosmic ripples that The First needed here.

- Note that The First only appeared in Buffy's life after Angel had returned from Hell. Possibly the entity was able to hitch a ride into this dimension in just this way.

- It is also notable that, in 'Amends', The First's initial attempts to influence Angel were *not* to have him kill himself, but merely to have him leave Sunnydale and then to kill Buffy and thus remove himself physically from her.

- Presumably, The First knew all about the prophecy of the vampire with a soul either stopping or, at least, having a significant part to play in an apocalypse and, therefore, wanted him out of the picture.

'SHE THINKS, THEREFORE I AM':
10 examples of the Zen-like thoughts of Daniel Osborne

Willow's boyfriend Oz is one of the most perplexing and intriguing characters in *Buffy*. Played with enigmatic brilliance by the great Seth Green, Oz can dominate scenes in which he had no dialogue with just little pieces of body language and a raised eyebrow. He's quiet and watchful most of the time, which means that on those occasions when he *does* speak it's usually worth listening to.

Oz's first appearance is in 'Inca Mummy Girl', admiring Willow's Eskimo costume at the fancy-dress party.

- What impresses Oz in a girl, he tells his bandmate Devon, involves a feather boa and 'The Theme from *A Summer Place*'.

- In 'What's My Line?' Part 2 he eats animal crackers (and has an interesting theory that the hippos are jealous because the monkeys all have pants).

- Despite being something of a computer expert and utterly brilliant at tests, Oz doesn't want a career. Instead his ambition is simply to play E flat diminished 9th on his Fender Stratocaster.

In 'Surprise' his relationship with Willow begins in the most charming way. Oz is sitting on the bench, practising with his guitar. Dingoes Ate My Baby are moving towards this brave new sound, he notes, then he confesses that, actually, they suck.

- Willow bets that Oz has lots of groupies. Oz, however, is living groupie-free.

- Oz tells Willow that he's going to ask her to go out. And he finds it interesting that he's nervous about it. Willow replies that, if it helps, she's going to say yes.

- This does, indeed, help. It creates a comfort zone.

- Willow suddenly remembers that Buffy's birthday party is tomorrow and blurts out that she can't. Oz likes the fact that Willow is unpredictable. Willow suggests that Oz come with her to the party and he accepts.

At the party the gang, who are waiting inside The Bronze to surprise Buffy, hear her fight with a vampire going on outside. Then Buffy and the vampire come crashing through a window. Buffy scrambles to her feet, grabs a drumstick and thrusts it into the vampire's chest just as Cordelia jumps up from behind the pool table shouting 'Surprise!' That, Oz notes, pretty much sums it up.

- He asks if everyone just saw that guy turn to dust. Xander explains that vampires are real and a lot of them live in Sunnydale.

- Oz realises that this actually explains a *lot*.

- From that moment onwards, Oz becomes a much-valued member of the Scooby Gang.

✎ Bitten on his finger by his young cousin Jordy, Oz discovers that he's going through some changes ('Phases'). He rings his Aunt Maureen and asks, casually, if Jordy is a werewolf?

- Desperate to keep his dreadful secret from Willow, Oz tries chaining himself up but Willow arrives just as he's transformed and Oz almost kills her.

- Buffy intervenes and also discovers that the murders, which had been attributed to the new werewolf in town, were actually the work of Angelus.

- Oz tells Willow that Giles has promised to let him use the book cage in the library to lock himself up around the full moon. He also humbly apologises for almost eating her.

- Willow is more disappointed that he didn't feel able to tell her.

- Willow agrees that it certainly is a complication but that it should in no way affect their relationship. Three days out of each month she isn't much fun to be around either.

✎ The abbreviated version of how Oz became a werewolf is told to Faith, in 'Faith, Hope and Trick'. It's a long story, notes Buffy. 'I got bit,' says Oz simply. Buffy reflects that, obviously, it's not *that* long.

✎ Oz may not say much a lot of the time but in 'Dead Man's Party' he gives a precise little essay on the differences between a gathering, a shindig and a hootenanny.

✎ Oz's relationship with Willow even survives the potential disaster of her kiss with Xander ('Lover's Walk').

- In 'Amends' the couple spend Christmas Eve together, alone at Willow's place. Willow has the room softly lit, with candles burning on the coffee table and Barry White's 'Can't Get Enough of Your Love, Babe' on the stereo.

- Oz isn't sure what to make of this and asks Willow if she ever has that dream where you're in the middle of a play and you don't know your lines or, indeed, the plot. (Of course, she subsequently does – see 'Restless'.)

- Willow intimates that she is ready to go to bed with him. Oz stands up suddenly. He isn't going; it was just a dramatic gesture.

- Willow wants Oz to be her first and says that she's ready, but he's not. Willow thought he had some experience in these matters. He has but this is different. When it happens, Oz wants it to be because they both need it.

- The couple finally sleep together in 'Graduation Day' Part 1.

Xander and Oz have an interesting friendship, bound together by a shared love of Willow. Note, for instance, the pair's incompetent attempts to rescue Willow and Buffy from the witch-burning in 'Gingerbread'.

- They discuss the essence of cool in 'The Zeppo'.

- They converse about the school's cheerleaders in 'Earshot' (Xander is quite a complex man, notes Oz pithily).

- When they prepare a spell for Willow, she leaves them a helpful diagram showing who has to do what, with stick-figure Oz differentiated from stick-figure Xander by having a little guitar ('Choices').

When Buffy gains telepathy ('Earshot'), she finally gets inside Oz's head. It's quite a Zen experience.

- I am my thoughts, Oz notes. If *they* exist in *her*, then Buffy contains everything that *is* me and she *becomes* me and I cease to exist. No one else exists either. Buffy is all of us. We think, therefore she is.

- Not only does he think in paraphrases of Rene Descartes, but some of Oz's thoughts are concepts straight out of Eastern philosophy and *Hsi Yu Chi*.

- But while Oz *thinks* a lot, he doesn't say much. While all of this is going on in his head, he sums it all up with just one spoken word: 'Hmm!'

At the UC Sunnydale Halloween fancy-dress party, Oz's costume is his normal clothes with a small sticker on his lapel saying GOD ('Fear Itself').

SLAYER

'MISTER I SPENT THE 60S IN AN ELECTRIC-KOOL-AND-FUNKY-SATAN-GROOVE':
The best of Rupert Giles's record collection
(… and the worst)

'Dear Sir, I have a twelve-inch piece of black plastic with a hole in the middle. Is this a record?'

He was once the bassist in a band ('The Dark Age') – even if, admittedly, he *wasn't* one of the original members of Pink Floyd ('Hush'). In his day, our Ripper was clearly a bit of a lad. 'In one episode I had a wind-up gramophone,' Tony Head has noted. 'Now I've got a proper system. Still vinyl, though, and quite right too … I'd love Giles to open a record shop.' But just what vinyl has Giles got hidden away in his cupboard? While it's possible to speculate that he may play battered copies of *Revolver*, *Exile on Main Street* or *London Calling* during those all-night research sessions, we've actually *seen* evidence of his inherent coolness.

Cream: *Disraeli Gears* (1967). Giles plays 'Tales of Brave Ulysses' for Joyce in 'Band Candy', and again in tribute to an almost perfect day spent with her, after her death in 'Forever'.

David Bowie: *Man of Words, Man of Music* (1969). 'Memory of a Free Festival' can be heard coming from Giles's stereo in 'The Freshman' when Buffy interrupts his and Olivia's long lie-in.

123

The Velvet Underground: *Loaded* (1970). In 'The Harsh Light of Day', when Oz enthuses over Giles's collection, Giles notes that there are actually more important things in life than records. Oz holds up a copy of the classic VU LP and asks, 'More important than *this*?' Even Giles is forced to concede the point in this particular instance.

The Who: *Who's Next* (1971), judging by his note-perfect rendition of 'Behind Blue Eyes' in The Espresso Pump in 'Where the Wild Things Are'.

David Bowie: *ChangesOneBowie* (1976). The distinctive cover of this bestselling compilation LP can be briefly glimpsed at the front of a stack of records in Giles's apartment during Xander and Spike's fight in 'Hush'.

However, like most of us, Rupert also has a few items that he probably hides away at the back.

The Bay City Rollers. Mentioned to Buffy as an example of proper music, in 'The Dark Age'. (On this occasion, he could have been joking.)

Lynard Skynard: *One More From The Road*. He's practising 'Free Bird' in 'The Yoko Factor'. All fifteen minutes of it. Never trust a hippy. Pass the ganja. Pass out.

Incidentally, younger *Buffy* fans may be interested to know that there was a genuine UK psych/prog band in the late 60s called Rupert's Children. They never had a hit.

TELEVISION, THE DRUG OF THE NATION

Classic TV shows referenced or alluded to in *Buffy* include:

- *Gidget* ('The Witch')

- *Star Trek* ('Nightmares', 'The Replacement')

- *Lost in Space* ('Out of Mind, Out of Sight')

- *Star Trek: The Next Generation* ('Prophecy Girl', 'Bring On the Night)

- *The Simpsons* ('Inca Mummy Girl', 'Older and Far Away')

- *The Prisoner* ('The Dark Age')

- *A Charlie Brown Christmas* ('Passion', 'The Replacement')

- *The Flintstones* ('Becoming' Part 2)

- *The Andy Griffiths Show* ('Faith, Hope and Trick', 'Villains')

- *Welcome Back Kotter* ('Band Candy')

- *Walker, Texas Ranger* ('The Zeppo')

- *The Patty Duke Show* ('This Year's Girl')

- *Felicity* ('Where the Wild Things Are')

- *The Fugitive* ('New Moon Rising')

- *The Banana Splits* ('Real Me')

- *Babylon 5* ('The Replacement')

- *Dawson's Creek* ('Out of my Mind', 'Chosen')

- *Friends* ('Triangle', 'Entropy')

- *Quantum Leap* ('Crush')

- *Xena: Warrior Princess* ('The Body', 'Conversations With Dead People')

- *Monty Python's Flying Circus* ('Spiral', 'The Gift', 'Villains', 'Him')

- *The Outer Limits* ('Spiral')

- *Charlie's Angels* ('All the Way')

- *Murder She Wrote* ('Smashed')

- *Ellen* ('Smashed')

- *I Dream of Jeannie* ('Dead Things')

- *HR Pufnstuff* ('All the Way', 'Seeing Red')

- *The Burns and Allen Show* ('Seeing Red')

- *Dragnet* ('Villains', 'Sleeper')

- *Alias* ('Beneath You')

- *Bewitched* ('Help')

- *Mission: Impossible* ('Him')

- *CSI: Crime Scene Investigations* ('Sleeper')

- *I, Claudius* ('End of Days')

- *I Love Lucy* ('End of Days')

STRANGE BEDFELLOWS:
The complicated psyche, lives and loves of Spike,
the second vampire with a soul – Part 6

Buffy believes that anyone dating a dead Harmony
Kendall must be, literally, the most tolerant guy in the world.
Spike and Harmony are the oddest of odd couples. In life,
Harmony was a ditsy, vacuous bitch princess (always in the
shadow of Sunnydale High's bitch queen, Cordelia Chase).
When she was sired by an anonymous vampire while fighting
the mayor on Graduation Day, she became a ditsy, vacuous
(and incompetent) vampire. Her subsequent attempt to command a gang of minions is truly hilarious ('Real Me').

Spike is still reeling from his break-up with Drusilla and
seems to be taking all his anger out on his new girlfriend. Yet
it is evident that he considers Harmony worthy of a dalliance
– she's certainly pretty. If only she would just *stop talking*.
Harmony is hooked on the notion of romantic love. Her lair
is all satin sheets and unicorn figurines, and she evidently rev-
els in her status as the girlfriend of Sunnydale's Big Bad. The
result is a relationship that goes beyond rebound and into
some very disturbing territory.

Harmony bites Willow and brags, proudly, that her
boyfriend is going to be mad that Oz and Willow were mean
to her. She uses baby-talk in front of Spike's minions. An infu-
riated Spike grabs Harmony and pins her against a wall.

Harmony, frankly, is aroused by the quasi-violence ('The Harsh Light of Day') – the first intimation that their relationship is based on some rather perverse psychology.

It's Harmony's whiny insistence on going to a party that leads to Spike running into Buffy and Buffy discovering that Spike is searching for The Gem of Amara. But Harmony isn't entirely the underdog in this relationship. She knows exactly which buttons to push to seduce Spike and, also, how to use his history with Drusilla to goad Spike into the type of S&M action that she enjoys. She isn't averse to a bit of mutual tongue biting. Spike, meanwhile, has cornered the market in withering put-downs – when Harmony accuses him of loving the tunnel that he's building more than her, he responds that, in fact, he loves *syphilis* more than her.

Spike finds the crypt that houses the gem and, maddened by Harmony's incessant chatter, stakes her. Which, since she's wearing the gem at the time, has no effect on her. Their relationship seems to be at an end.

The pair meet again when Spike, rendered incapable of hunting by the electronic chip in his head, goes to Harmony for help. Harmony is, initially, interested in reviving their relationship. Until, that is, he starts talking about killing the Slayer. Hell has no fury like a woman scorned. Harmony takes her revenge in the most brutal way. We all know Spike hurt her feelings, but burning his Sex Pistols CDs …? That's just *mean*.

When Spike attempts again to get her help, he's given a lecture on female empowerment. Harmony declares herself to be powerful and beautiful and in no need of a man to complete her. Spike, in desperation, turns to the Scoobies,

129

offering information about The Initiative in return for protection and food ('Pangs'). Later, when Spike's uneasy partnership with the Scooby Gang is well established, Harmony, rejected and threatened by her gang of minions, comes to Spike for help – offering to do *absolutely anything* for him in return. This includes the resumption of their sexual relationship, which she spells out for him just in case there's any misunderstanding on Spike's part about just *exactly* how desperate she is.

Harmony tries to be supportive of Spike – she knows how sensitive he is ('Fool for Love') – but his growing preoccupation with Buffy is by this stage moving into dark waters. He uses a Buffy mannequin to work out his aggression ('Out of my Mind'). Following a dream revelation that he is, actually, in love with the Slayer, he may be busy bedding Harmony but his fantasies mean he's *thinking* about Buffy ('Family'). This leads to a spot of role-play. Harmony, keen to rekindle the passion in her rocky relationship, has no objections to donning Buffy's cashmere sweater and stalking her errant lover in a suggestive manner, much to Spike's evident satisfaction.

When Drusilla arrives back in Sunnydale, in 'Crush', Harmony thinks it's just another kink. She and Spike have evidently discussed the possibilities of a threesome and Harmony has made it clear that she's only interested in boy/boy/girl (unless actress Charlize Theron is involved), especially as Spike's chosen seems to be some pick-up dressed like his ex. When Harmony realises that this pick-up *is* actually Drusilla, she delivers an impassioned speech about how she's had to support Spike through the emotional turmoil that Dru left him in. (Drusilla's face when Harmony refers to Spike as 'Boo Boo' is *priceless*.)

It's hard not to feel sorry for poor Harmony when Spike dismisses her. And leave she does, only to return with a crossbow. Spike can complain all he likes that women are just bitches who set out to torture him but, in this case, he doesn't deserve an ounce of sympathy.

'COLLEGE NOT SO SCARY AFTER ALL?':
12 great lines of dialogue from *Buffy*'s Season 4

Xander's finest hour: 'When it's dark and I'm alone and I'm scared or freaked out … I always think, "What would Buffy do?" You're my hero.' – 'The Freshman'

Xander, when Anya suggests that they have sex: 'What you're talking about, and I'm actually turning into a woman as I say this, but it's about expressing something. Accepting consequences.' Anya: 'I have condoms. Some are black.' – 'The Harsh Light of Day'

Spike, assuming that The Initiative is Buffy's work: 'I always worried what would happen when that bitch got some funding.' – 'The Initiative'

Xander, while the others have a lengthy conversation about political correctness: 'Can we come rocketing back to the part about me and my new syphilis?' – 'Pangs'

Xander, told that Buffy and Spike are getting married: 'How? What? How?' Giles: 'Three excellent questions.' – 'Something Blue'

Riley: 'Tell me about your dream. As a Psych major, I'm qualified to go "hmm".' – 'Hush'

🗡 Ethan Rayne, regretfully: 'I've really got to learn to just do the damage and get out of town. It's the "stay and gloat" that gets me every time.' – 'A New Man'

🗡 Giles, on The Initiative's tracer: 'It's blinking.' Spike: 'I don't care if it's playing "Rockin' the Casbah" on the bloody Jew's harp, just get it out of me.' – 'The I in Team'

🗡 Buffy, entering The Initiative's complex: 'I'm the only one that can pass the retinal scan.' Xander: 'Eww. I don't wanna see *that*.' Buffy: '*Retinal. Scan.*' – 'Goodbye Iowa'

🗡 Giles: 'I know what you're going to say ...' Faith: 'I'm Buffy.' Giles: 'All right, I *didn't* know what you were going to say.' – 'Who's That Girl?'

🗡 Buffy, on Jonathan: 'He starred in *The Matrix* but he never left town. And how'd he graduate from med school? He's only eighteen years old.' Xander: 'Effective time management?' – 'Superstar'

🗡 Xander, on Willow: 'She does *spells* with Tara ... Sometimes I think about two women doing *a spell*. And then I do a spell *by myself*.' – 'Restless'

LOGIC, LET ME INTRODUCE YOU TO THIS WINDOW:

10 more things in *Buffy the Vampire Slayer* that make absolutely no logical sense whatsoever

✎ Vampires in general, and Spike in particular, are at pains *not* to see the end of the world – for a variety of reasons, not least being that they like feeding from humans ('Becoming' Part 2). That renders the entire resurrection of The Judge to bring forth Armageddon plot (in 'Surprise' and 'Innocence') somewhat pointless.

✎ The Guardian says that she wants to protect Buffy ('End of Days'). So where, exactly, has she been for the last seven years during the events of various apocalyptic earth-shattering disasters?

- Where was she, for instance, when Buffy twice died ('Prophecy Girl', 'The Gift')?

- Considering that The Guardian has been hidden since the time of the Shadow Men and the first Slayer, she speaks remarkably good English (complete with modern slang expressions like 'nope').

- The weapon (described by several characters as a scythe even though it's clearly an axe) is said to have been forged

134

centuries ago. Shouldn't that be *millennia* if it's a pre-Christian artefact?

- That brings up the question of when, exactly, the weapon was made and what it was made from. If its creation was at 'the dawn of civilisation' – say 3,000 BC – then it is unlikely to be iron as no one knew how to forge such a metal at that time.

- We have an artefact being created in the known ancient world (in the weapon's case, the Nile Delta of Egypt) and then, in some unexplained way, being transported to America, which wouldn't even be discovered by the rest of the world for another 4,500 years. Who took it there? How did they know that they wouldn't fall off the end of the world?

- Why are the two Hellmouths that we know about – Sunnydale and Cleveland – *both* on a continent that, until 1492, only the indigenous population and, allegedly, a few lost vikings had any knowledge of?

- We have the same problem with The Gem of Amara in 'The Harsh Light of Day'. Giles notes that there was much vampiric interest in locating The Gem during the tenth century. Vampires combed the earth but no one found it. Hardly surprising since it was buried on a continent undiscovered by Westerners until 400 years later.

Modern Sunnydale was founded in 1900 by Richard Wilkins (although there was a prior Spanish settlement from the 1700s alluded to in 'The Harvest' and 'Pangs'). If, as Wilkins suggests, he set up Sunnydale as a demon feeding ground, then is *he* responsible for Buffy being there also?

135

- Consider the numerous occasions when world-threatening situations were only averted directly because Buffy was on hand to stop them – The Master, The Judge, Acathla and the Hellmouth creature seen in 'The Zeppo' are all potential Armageddon-type scenarios.

- 'Homecoming' and 'Lover's Walk' both indicate that the Mayor had full knowledge of more or less everything that was going on in Sunnydale during the two years prior to his introduction, so one has to wonder if there was something in the way that he created the town which meant that such apocalypses would always fail, or if he was depending on Buffy and her friends all along?

According to some eagle-eyed fans, the rat used to portray Amy in 'Something Blue' and 'Doomed' was a male.

Spike has a television in his mausoleum where one wouldn't normally expect an electricity supply to be ('Goodbye Iowa').

In 'The Harvest', Giles is highly dismissive of Christianity, describing it as 'popular mythology'. However, Judaeo-Christian symbols such as the crucifix and holy water are still deadly to a vampire, and a plethora of biblical lore is quoted within the series (note, for instance, Spike's reference to Christ's crucifixion as an actual historical event in 'School Hard').

Buffy has three separate birthdays in the series: two (24 October 1980 and 6 May 1979) appear on computer records in the same episode – 'I, Robot … You, Jane'. The third is never specifically confirmed but, from evidence in 'The Puppet Show', 'Surprise', 'Helpless', 'The Gift' and 'Older and Far Away', the best guess would be during the third week of January 1981.

As in many modern television shows, there is an extremely naïve correlation in *Buffy* between the Internet and sources of all knowledge (notably in 'I, Robot … You, Jane', but also in other episodes). Confidential information is seldom, if ever, stored on the Internet directly *because* it can be accessed by anyone.

As part of his campaign to get Buffy expelled, Principal Snyder on several occasions describes her as the worst student in the school. Some of the faculty's other teaching staff seem to have a similarly low opinion of her. Why, exactly?

- 'I, Robot … You, Jane' confirms that Buffy's Grade Point Average is 2.8. While not exactly in Willow's league, this still corresponds to C+ or B- level.

- Buffy's SAT scores are even more impressive ('Lover's Walk').

- If Snyder is merely talking about Buffy being a disruptive influence to other students, in a school that contains hooligans as obnoxious as Sheila ('School Hard'), Rodney Munson ('Inca Mummy Girl'), Jack O'Toole ('The Zeppo'), Larry ('Phases') and Gage Petronzi ('Go Fish'), does anyone really think she's *that* bad?

Watch closely the scene in the library in 'Bad Eggs' when Buffy puts her experimental egg on Giles's desk close to a chain. The respective positions of the chain and the egg change from shot to shot about four times. It's so obvious that one almost suspects it was done deliberately to provide books like this with something to talk about.

137

A LITTLE LEARNING IS A DANGEROUS THING:
10 moments when *Buffy the Vampire Slayer* characters reveal the inadequacies of their education

Cordelia once noted that she didn't believe anyone should be made to do anything educational in school if they don't want to. In Sunnydale, seemingly, any form of imparted knowledge is an optional extra to staying alive. Any education that the kids of Sunnydale High manage to get out of Ms Jackson's English class or Mr Miller's history lectures is purely coincidental.

Xander tells Willow that he has a problem with the math. When she asks which part, he merely repeats, 'the math' ('Welcome to the Hellmouth').

- Willow's attempts to teach Xander basic geometry are hindered by him being possessed ('The Pack').

- Xander is surprised to discover that spiders are arachnids and, therefore, from the Middle East ('Nightmares').

- He has difficulty working out what B-I-T-C-H spells ('When She Was Bad').

- He doesn't know who drafted the Constitution ('Go Fish').

- He thinks that four times five is thirty ('Earshot').

When asked by the murderous Jack O'Toole if he's retarded, Xander notes that he had to take a test when he was seven. This established that, while he's a little slow in math and spatial relations, he is certainly not challenged ('The Zeppo').

Buffy is worried – in 'Some Assembly Required' – that Slaying is interfering with her trigonometry homework. She also notes that she's repressed pretty much anything math-related ('I Only Have Eyes For You'). It's nice to discover that repression somewhat runs in her family.

Willow helps the inordinately stupid Rodney Munson with his chemistry homework ('Inca Mummy Girl'). He says that he's almost memorised the fourteen natural elements. Willow, sadly, informs him that there are actually 103. (However, she's wrong. Since the discovery of the 103rd – Lawrencium in 1961 – a further eight had been identified by 1998.)

Other hopeless educational cases whom Willow gets lumbered with helping by Principal Snyder include:

- Gage Petronzi ('Go Fish')

- Basketball superstar Percy West ('Doppelgängland')

She does, however, seem to enjoy teaching those who actually want to learn ('Passion').

Snyder's preconditions for the expelled Buffy to become a schoolgirl again are that she takes make-up tests on all the classes she skipped last year, providing a letter of recommendation from a member of the faculty who isn't an English librarian ('Faith, Hope and Trick') and seeing the school psychologist ('Beauty and the Beasts'). She eventually passes all the exams, although her reaction to an English test (asking, in all seriousness, if they give you a credit for speaking it) does make one wonder how.

🖋 Amy uses her recently acquired magical skills to con Ms Beakman into believing that she has handed in a test paper, which, in reality, she hasn't ('Bewitched, Bothered and Bewildered').

🖋 Willow notes that Oz is the highest-scoring person on SATs never to graduate. It's unclear whether she's talking about just Sunnydale High or the whole country. Xander adds that he's against any system that discriminates against the uninformed ('Band Candy').

- Willow's SAT score for English Verbal of 740 (she's hugely disappointed with this, comparing herself with *The Simpsons*' Cletus the Slack-Jawed Yokel) is more than both of Xander's scores added together.

- The maximum SAT score in Verbal is 800; the maximum combined score is 1,600. Buffy's combined score, 1,430, surprises not only everyone else, but also herself.

- Cordelia also seems to have done well – as she predicted that she would ('Lover's Walk').

🖋 Cordelia, when researching an English paper, says that she wants Wesley's help … because he's English ('Enemies').

🖋 Harmony is surprised when told by Willow that they have museums in France ('The Harsh Light of Day'). In terms of languages she, seemingly, also doesn't know the difference between French and Italian ('The Initiative').

Buffy and Willow discuss aspects of the French Revolution, including Jean-Paul Marat (1743–93, author of *The Chains of Slavery*), Charlotte Corday (a Girondin supporter who murdered Marat in his bath) and Maximilien-François Robespierre (1758–94, the Jacobin leader and instigator of The Reign of Terror). Buffy, however, fails to spot Willow's witty allusion to the occipital lobe ('Out of my Mind').

Anya says it's a myth that Santa Claus is a myth. He's been around since the 1500s. He wasn't always called Santa, of course, but Christmas night, flying reindeer, coming down the chimney … all of that is true. Of course, he doesn't traditionally bring presents so much as disembowel naughty children ('The Body').

SLAYER

OUCH!:
10 moments of severe cranial trauma for Rupert Giles

Poor old Giles: even before he was reduced to a wounded dwarf with the mystical strength of a doily ('Chosen') this erudite Watcher, who speaks five languages, managed to get his noggin in the way of heavy objects with alarming regularity. It's no wonder that he once defined himself as 'an unemployed librarian with a tendency to get knocked on the head' ('A New Man'). Even if there's no one around to render him unconscious, Giles is still capable of getting the job done all by himself. On one occasion, distracted by Buffy's discovery that he's had sex with her mother, he gets out of an embarrassing situation by walking into a tree and, presumably, the welcoming arms of oblivion ('Earshot').

Of course, Giles's capacity for attracting disaster isn't merely limited to head injuries. He has also:

- Been chloroformed ('Gingerbread').

- Been impaled on a lance ('Spiral').

- Fallen into an open grave ('All the Way').

- Been shot with his own tranquilliser gun ('Beauty and The Beasts').

Let's have a look at some of the more painful of these mishaps. And, maybe, take an aspirin in sympathy.

'Prophecy Girl': Giles is knocked out by Buffy in order to stop him from taking her place and probably getting killed by The Master. She feels bad about it though, leaving Jenny Calendar to tend to the invalid, with instructions that she should make up something cool to tell him when he wakes up and say that Buffy said it.

'Inca Mummy Girl': Giles is rendered unconscious by Ampatha in the Sunnydale museum.

'The Dark Ages': Giles is punched round his sitting room, then has his head repeatedly slammed on his desk by the demon Eyghon, who happens to be in possession of his girlfriend's body.

'Passion': Heartbroken by the murder of Jenny, Giles decides to attack Angelus in his lair. One spot of ultraviolence later, Giles is rendered unconscious and has to be dragged from the burning building by Buffy, who promptly clouts him again for good measure before comforting him in his grief.

'Becoming' Part 1: As Giles and Willow attempt to perform a ritual that will give Angelus his soul back, their chanting is interrupted by Drusilla and her minions. Giles is swiftly knocked out and taken back to the mansion for a spot of physical and psychological torture.

'Gingerbread': Having been rendered unconscious by the minions of MOO (Mothers Against the Occult), Giles is rescued by Cordelia who wakes him up with a few slaps to the head and a speech about his alarming propensity for getting

143

knocked out. Having warned him that one of these days he's going to wake up in a coma, Cordy interprets his babblings about Hansel and Gretel as a sign of brain damage, and is at pains to stress that this happened *before* she hit him.

'Revelations': Treacherous Watcher Gwendolyn Post uses a wooden statue to deliver such a thunderous whack on Giles's bonce that he's wheeled out of the library on a stretcher, apparently fighting for his life.

'Pangs': Attacked in his home by vengeful Chumash warriors, Giles cleverly manages to avoid outright oblivion.

'Doomed': Giles is beaten by three Vahrall demons in search of The Word of Valios, which Giles happens to have in a box of mystical knick-knacks.

'Flooded': Returning from England to greet his resurrected Slayer, Giles is made to feel right at home when the demon M'Fashnik knocks him through a staircase. As he sits with the inevitable ice pack clutched to his face, Giles muses that, at least now he's been knocked unconscious, he knows that he's back in America.

SLAYER

'BIKES, SKATEBOARDS AND AUTOMOBILES':
14 methods of transportation as used by
characters in *Buffy*

Joyce Summers owns a typical soccer-mom-mobile, a Jeep Cherokee Sport ('Welcome to the Hellmouth'). Buffy's first opportunity to drive it comes in somewhat catastrophic circumstances ('Band Candy') and ends with a large repair bill.

Xander's initial mode of transport is a skateboard ('Welcome to the Hellmouth'). His handling skills leave something to be desired. Later, he borrows his Uncle Rory's car ('The Zeppo'), a light green 1957 Chevrolet Bel Air. He subsequently gets a car of his own, a nice red Subaru (first seen in 'The Body'). Willow destroys this to delay Buffy from getting to the town jail in order to stop her from killing Jonathan and Andrew ('Two To Go'). Xander does what any sensible lawabiding citizen would, and steals a police car. A few months later ('Lessons'), he's bought a new silver Merc (3 PCE 187).

Giles's first car is a 1963 Citröen DS Coupé, a classic motor that had fallen somewhat into disrepair ('The Witch'). Once this is destroyed by Spike ('A New Man'), Giles replaces it with a red sporty BMW 328 iC with automatic transmission and a very loud stereo ('Real Me').

Spike's 'deathmobile' is a 1963 DeSoto ('School Hard'). When he and Buffy stake out a group of alleged vampires

145

('Crush'), Spike tries to be personable by humming the Ramones' 'I Wanna Be Sedated'. As Buffy had previously noted, however, she can't stand guys who hum ('Helpless').

Cordelia's car is a flashy red Chrysler Sebring convertible with the licence plate 'QUEEN C' ('Reptile Boy').

The zebra-striped van that Oz drives in 'Halloween' has the steering wheel on the right, which suggests that it's British-made. He appears to have replaced this with a tan lefthand-drive model by 'Innocence'.

The Maclays have a rather battered camper van, which could be used as an example of regionalist stereotyping if the viewer was of a bigoted disposition ('Family').

Spike steals a decrepit Winnebago as the Scooby Gang's getaway vehicle ('Spiral'). Giles says that he's driven tricycles with more power. Spike wanted to obtain a Porsche but, unfortunately, they only seat two people.

Spike obtains one of the motorbikes from the gang of rampaging demon-bikers who berserk their way through Sunnydale ('Bargaining' Part 1). It becomes his regular mode of transport for the next couple of years. On occasions he carries pillion passengers, like Dawn and Andrew.

When being chased by a demon, Willow and Dawn leap into a convenient car, which Willow magically commands to drive off. And crashes, resulting in a broken arm for Dawn ('Smashed').

During the stock footage of London seen in 'Sleeper', two black taxis and a red Nissan Micra (W291 LHU) appear. If the latter is *your* car, please write to the production office and claim your royalties instantly.

Caleb drives a battered old Ford pick-up ('Dirty Girls').

Clem drives a red VW Beetle ('Touched').

The gang's getaway vehicle from the destruction of Sunnydale is a yellow school bus ('Chosen').

'DEATH IS YOUR GIFT':
12 great lines of dialogue from *Buffy*'s Season 5

Dawn, on Willow and Tara: 'I told Mom one time I wished they'd teach me some of the things they do together. Then she got really quiet and made me go upstairs.' – 'Real Me'

Riley, on the two Xanders: 'Psychologically, this is fascinating. Doesn't it make everyone wanna lock them in separate rooms and do experiments on them? Just me then?' – 'The Replacement'

Spike, when Buffy asks him for an explanation of what he's doing outside her house in five words or less: 'Out. For. A. Walk. Bitch.' – 'No Place Like Home'

Buffy: 'You think we're dancing?' Spike: 'That's all we've ever done.' – 'Fool for Love'

Willow, upon finding the extraterrestrial snot-monster: 'We're experienced.' Anya: 'Yes, it seems like we're always dealing with creatures from outer space. Except that we don't ever do that!' – 'Listening to Fear'

Buffy: 'I killed something in a convent last night.' Xander: 'In any other room, a frightening declaration. Here, a welcome distraction.' – 'Triangle'

Nigel: 'Magical proficiency level?' Willow: 'High. Very high. One of those top levels.' Tara, panicking: 'Five!' – 'Checkpoint'

Buffy, after April has thrown her across the room: 'I've had it with super-strong little women who aren't me.' – 'I Was Made to Love You'

Anya, on Joyce's death: 'I don't understand how this all happens. How we go through this. I knew her, and then she's just a body.' – 'The Body'

The Buffybot's Spike-influenced comment on his love-rival: 'Angel's lame. His hair grows straight up and he's *bloody stupid*.' – 'Intervention'

Glory, on Spike: 'What the hell is *that*, and why is his hair that colour?' – 'Intervention'

Spike, to Buffy: 'I know you'll never love me. I know that I'm a monster. But you treat me like a man.' – 'The Gift'

WHAT'S ON IN SUNNYDALE?:
6 places to visit if you happen to find yourself in California's best-kept secret (population 38,000 ... and falling)

Now it's just a big hole in the ground where once there was a town, but Sunnydale used to get the odd tourist. The following is reproduced from the local publication *What's On In Sunnydale*. (It's a bit of paper with 'NAFF ALL' written on it.)

 The miniature-golf course ('Ted', 'Enemies').

 The Sun Cinema. Which still appeared to be showing *Dude, Where's My Car?* two years after that movie had closed everywhere else ('Bargaining' Part 1).

 The Espresso Pump. Where you can pay good money to hear Rupert Giles singing maudlin hippy anthems ('Where the Wild Things Are', 'The Yoko Factor').

 The Bronze. Where you will be guaranteed a good night out. Unless there's a vampire attack. Or a troll attack. Or a werewolf attack. The food's good though – particularly the onion-flower thingy so beloved by Spike ('Triangle').

150

The exclusive, if nameless, restaurant hidden down a back alley ('First Date'). So long as you avoid finding *yourself* as an item on the menu.

The Mall ('Bad Eggs', 'Innocence', 'Chosen'). Where, according to Giles, the sales staff are rude and everything in the food court is sticky.

MADNESS IS JUST A STATE OF MIND:
The complicated psyche, lives and loves of Spike,
the second vampire with a soul – Part 7

When Spike returns to Sunnydale after enduring unspeakable
torment in order to regain his soul ('Two To Go', 'Grave'), he
is, to put it bluntly, off his rocker. Living in the haunted, wall-
shifting First-infested basement of Sunnydale High doesn't
help. But listen carefully to his insane burblings and there *is* a
core of logic in there somewhere, struggling for freedom.

In 'Lessons', Spike greets Buffy with surprise and then a
tender 'duck'. Not an endearment, just an instruction to avoid
a metal pipe that's about to hit her on the … oops, too late.
However, he's still *compos mentis* enough to identify Buffy's
zombie-ghost problem. A child of four could figure it out, he
notes. Mind you, the child William seemed more likely to
have been wearing a dunce's hat and sitting in a corner, not
being a quick study it seems. And clumsy too, dropping his
slate in the water so the chalk ran.

Spike had a speech all planned but Buffy won't (or can't)
understand it. As Spike is visited by faces from his past it's
clear what's in store for both him and Sunnydale. The First is
back in town and Spike seems to be its initial target. It's difficult to see where the insanity ends and possession by The First
begins. There will be no redemptive Christmas miracle for
him, unlike Angel ('Amends'). It's going to be a long road

back to sanity, and first there's the baggage left over from his exit from Sunnydale ('Seeing Red') to deal with.

When Spike walks into Buffy's sitting room ('Beneath You'), the wild hair has been replaced by his usual bleached locks. He seems to be sane again, talking sensibly, offering to help. He shakes off Xander's pointed hostility (though Dawn's venom at the man who tried to rape her sister takes him by surprise). Yet he knows that he has done something that cannot be simply forgiven – words like sorry are of no use in this situation. All he can do is tell Buffy that he has changed and try to move on. Buffy accepts that he has changed; she's just not sure into what.

It's Spike who identifies the monster (a wormlike Sluggoth demon). Spike then heads out over the rooftops to slay the beast. Sadly for him, just as Spike skewers the transformed Ronnie, Anya releases him from her spell, turning him back into the abusive, albeit human, bastard of a boyfriend. The pain from The Initiative chip and the realisation of what he's done hits Spike, and the only way he can deal with this emotionally is to revert into madness. He gets it together long enough to let Buffy know (about the biggest of Big Bads) that everything is going to collapse in screaming blood and horror then, with a final warning of 'from beneath you, it devours', he legs it into one of Sunnydale's many redundant churches.

He pours out the story of his remorse at having been used as a convenient sex object. A horrified Buffy asks if Spike has completely lost his mind and gets a surprisingly sensible response. Buffy listens as Spike rambles on about sparks and burning, and works out that the vampire has his soul back. A soul that's filling his head with ghosts and driving him insane. He did it, he says, to be the kind of man who would never do

153

the things that Spike once did to Buffy. He rails against Angel for not telling him of the consequences. Souled or unsouled, he is now – and forever – a fool for love. All he wants is to be forgiven and loved. As he drapes his body over a cross, burns himself and pleads for rest, Buffy flees (though, thankfully, she seems to have got him off the cross before she disappears).

Spike helps Buffy fight off a demon and a gang of schoolboys ('Help'). He tries to find some redemption in saving another girl from being hurt, even though he himself is guilty of hurting Buffy. Remorse and a determination to help the girl drive him to ignore the pain of his behavioural chip. His reward comes when the girl he helped to save gives him a crumb of hope, telling him that one day Buffy *will* tell him that she loves him. Sadly, when she does ('Chosen'), he doesn't believe her.

In 'Selfless', a surprisingly sympathetic Buffy listens to Spike rambling about how he can no longer trust what he sees. Buffy offers to help, reassuring Spike that they will get through this together. Sadly, this is another First-induced hallucination. The real Buffy is much tougher but more pragmatic. She realises that it's the basement that makes Spike crazy. Buffy persuades a very reluctant Xander to take Spike in and keep him in his closet ('Him').

WHO'S THE HARDEST?:

If all of the main villains from *Buffy the Vampire Slayer* had a massive fight, which of them would win?

The Master: A bit of a dark horse. Aged and very powerful, and with a cool line in sarcastic comments and eye-gouging. Limited, as all vampires are, by the usual sunlight-related problems.

Spike and Drusilla: Cunning, vicious, not to be messed with, Sunnydale's Sid and Nancy would be a match for most other Big Bads, particularly if you take Drusilla's gift of second sight into account. However, Dru also suffers from awkward mental instability and the couple's close relationship with each other is a definite limitation in a dogfight situation, particularly if Angelus is thrown into the mix. Plus, of course, Spike's record as a Big Bad in Sunnydale is not at all good – he always seems to get his ass kicked, usually by Buffy. Nevertheless, Spike and Dru have, between them, killed three Slayers – that's three more than the rest of the Big Bads put together.

Angelus: Dangerous. Knows how to press all the right buttons to make The Master and, subsequently, Spike lose their tempers. Can charm the pants off any passing Slayer (quite literally in one particular case). Flawed by his soul and his rank embarrassment at what a right girly-man Angel is. When

Angelus is driving the body, however, uh-oh, look out. A definite contender. He's also, easily, the funniest of the assembled contestants.

Mayor Richard Wilkins III: Probably too nice to win a race like this. Wilkins's problem is that, at heart, he's a decent, hardworking example of conservative small-town American sensibilities – as out of place in the 1990s as The Master is. Richard comes from a simpler time – full of family values, the work ethic, mom's apple pie and *Leave It To Beaver*. That's why he's such a refreshing change for Faith from the cynical and deceitful world that she finds herself a part of in Sunnydale. He might be evil but at least he'll never let you down. Not adverse to the odd deranged act of ultraviolence, immortal until ascended and, once ascended, a VERY BIG SNAKE. But still, ultimately, too one-dimensional to challenge the really big hitters.

Adam: Aesthetically a clear loser, but this isn't a beauty contest. Adam's incredible strength and super-intelligence set him ahead of most of his rivals but he is fatally flawed by linear and overly logical thinking. Put simply, most of the other Big Bads might have guessed that Buffy, Xander, Giles and Willow would try something as insanely dangerous as summoning the essence of the first Slayer to defeat them. Adam, on the other hand, missed that one completely and, when confronted with an Über-Slayer, didn't have any answer to her.

Glory: In theory, Glory should wipe the floor with the rest of the opposition. She's a frikkin' god, for heaven's sake. However, therein lies her problem. Glory is only powerful when she's in her own body. When Ben's in charge, he/she is just a human without any inherent strength, power or skills (apart from an ability to summon Queller demons). That's how Buffy and her friends defeated her in 'The Gift' after so many outrageous pummellings during previous episodes; just wait until Ben takes over and, as he does, Giles puts his lights out. That's a pretty severe flaw for a pan-dimensional goddess.

The *Troika*: Absolutely *the* guys if you desperately need to know the name of Mr Spock's mother for a forthcoming trivia quiz. Otherwise, forget 'em, especially in anything resembling a fight.

Evil Willow: Ah, *now* we're talking. At last somebody who could really give Angelus a run for his money. Inhibited only by Willow's basic goodness, when the twin evils of magic addiction and dark power come together, particularly if there's a catalyst like revenge involved, then we are talking some serious mojo. Evil Willow's got pretty much everything – arcane knowledge, strength of bitterness, the pithy asides. Plus, she looks *really* hot (albeit, you know, a bit gothy) in the black gear. A combination of serious dominatrix vibe, the Wicked Witch of the West and John Wayne in *The Searchers*, here is someone that you, literally, don't want to mess with.

The First: Technically, The First inhabits the power of all of the above and then some, a collective vessel for all of the horrors that the world has ever known and ever will know. The First is everlasting, hard as nails and will wait for an eternity for its chance to strike. Its shape-changing abilities are useful and scary, and it has plenty of minions to do much of its leg work. The only problem, really, is in its non-corporealness. And, also, in the fact that it has to talk its victims to death. Even though The First is very good at this, time could be a factor in this game.

157

The likely result: If Glory can maintain her godlike form, she's the winner. If not, then it's a straight fight between Angelus and Evil Willow and, frankly, too close to call. Just, you know, stay the hell away from wherever it is that the fight is happening.

'WEST HOLLYWOOD!':
The 5 gayest moments in *Buffy the Vampire Slayer*

'I think part of the attraction of the *Buffy*verse [is that] it lends itself to polymorphously perverse subtext,' Joss Whedon once noted on the *Buffy Posting Board*. 'I personally find romance in every relationship. I love all the characters, so I say Bring Your Own Subtext!' So, people took him at his word.

Xander and Larry: Believing that Larry, the school's clichéd bully-boy jock, is the werewolf who has been terrorising Sunnydale, Xander goes to the locker room to confront his nemesis ('Phases').

- Xander doesn't react with fear to Larry's threats and tells the big guy that he knows what he has been doing at nights.

- Larry wonders if this is a blackmail attempt, but Xander just wants to help. 'You think you have a *cure*?' asks Larry incredulously.

- Xander, reflecting on his own experiences of Hyena-possession ('The Pack'), says that he's been there.

- Such options are easy for Xander, Larry notes. He is, after all, *nobody*. Larry, on the other hand, has a reputation. How are people going to treat him after they find out that he's gay?

- Larry appears as if a heavy burden has been lifted from him. He repeats that he's gay and Xander, nervously backing away, replies that he heard the first time.

- Larry reflects that Xander, of all people, brought it out of him. Knowing that Xander went through the same thing made it easier for Larry to admit it.

- Xander stammers that he himself is not ... you know ... 'Of course,' says Larry sympathetically. 'Don't worry, your secret is safe with me.'

- Later, when Buffy discovers that there is a would-be assassin on campus ('Earshot'), Xander again approaches Larry and notes that it must be frustrating to have a secret.

- Larry laughs and notes that he's so 'Out' his grandma is fixing him up on dates with guys.

- However, Larry thinks that it sounds as though Xander himself is having a rough time. Just do it, Larry advises. Have a word with Freddy Iverson at the school paper, and put a 'Coming-Out' announcement in the next edition. Something tasteful.

Willow and Tara: A friendship that begins through mutual scorn of Wanna-Blessed-Bes and some hand-holding ('Hush'), Willow and Tara soon discover that they have more in common than simply both being practising witches.

- Their relationship soon becomes far more intimate, floating a rose with surprisingly erotic results ('A New Man').

- Faith, inhabiting Buffy's body, is the first person to spot that the girls have become an item ('Who Are You?').

- Willow doesn't tell Buffy, Xander and Giles until they are in a blazing row about how to tackle Adam's apocalyptic schemes ('The Yoko Factor').

- Tara becomes a trusted and much-loved member of the Scooby Gang.

- This is especially evident in 'Family', where her friends rescue Tara from the depressing prospect of returning home to a life of drab servitude. The episode ends with Willow and Tara, literally, dancing on air.

Xander and Spike: As Nancy is introduced to the various people who are going to help her, she gleams that their inter-relationships have a somewhat complex history. So, let's get this straight: Buffy once went with Spike; Spike once went with Anya; Anya once went with Xander? 'Is there anyone here who *hasn't* slept together?' she asks. Xander and Spike look at each other awkwardly ('Beneath You').

Willow and Kennedy: Saucy rich-girl potential Slayer Kennedy arrives with Giles, along with two other girls. She persuades Willow that she would make a much better room-mate than Molly (who chatters incessantly) or Annabelle (who snores). Then, flirtatiously, Kennedy says that Willow better not hog the covers ('Bring On the Night').

- The more minxy dom/sub aspects of Kennedy's sexual pursuit of Willow are particularly noticeable in 'Showtime', a radical juxtaposition to the lengthy and tender build-up to Willow and Tara's first kiss ('The Body').

161

- When Willow and Kennedy kiss ('The Killer in Me'), the repressed guilt and rage inside Willow over what she did to Warren ('Villains'), and her belief that by kissing another woman she is, effectively, accepting Tara's death, turns Willow into the man that she killed. It takes Kennedy's belief in her to bring her back.

- Kennedy and Willow finally get down to some in-bed naughtiness and neck-licking, and the noise they make makes Anya so jealous that she and Xander end up writhing around on the kitchen floor in protest ('Touched').

Xander and Andrew: There are some slyly homoerotic allusions concerning Andrew and Xander – in 'Showtime' – concerning Andrew's joystick hand. Subsequently, after returning home from his disastrous date with Lissa, Xander begs Willow to make him gay in a bizarre rant that seems to arouse Andrew as soon as actor Scott Bacula's name is mentioned ('First Date'). When Willow and Kennedy are, very visibly, making out on the couch, Andrew is much more interested in pointing his camera at the replacement windows, which Xander previously fitted. And on observing what a good job Xander did on them and how talented he is ('Storyteller').

DEUS EX MACHINA:
10 magical MacGuffins that suddenly appear in the *Buffy* universe without pre-warning

Director Alfred Hitchcock once told a story about a man who was sitting on a train, opposite someone who had a small cage in which was some obviously ferocious animal. 'What's in the cage?' the man asked. 'A MacGuffin,' came the reply. 'It's to catch all of the lions on the Scottish moors.' The man thought about this for a moment. 'But there are *no* lions on the Scottish moors,' he noted. 'In that case,' his new acquaintance replied, 'that is *no* MacGuffin.'

Deus Ex Machina (literal Latin translation: 'a God out of a machine') means any wholly unlikely device in drama serving the sole purpose of moving the plot along to provide resolution. A MacGuffin, in other words. Like most dramas, *Buffy* features its fair share of these:

The Mark of Gachnar ('Fear Itself'): After an accident involving Oz's blood and a demonic symbol painted on a frat-house floor, the Scooby Gang find themselves trapped in a Halloween house of horrors while Gachnar, the fear demon, feeds on their hidden terrors. Luckily, Gachnar, while big on angst is pretty small in all other respects.

The Glove of Myneghon ('Revelations'): When Faith's new Watcher, Gwendolyn Post (Mrs), arrives in town, she sets the Slayers a task: to find The Glove of Myneghon before the demon Lagos can get his hands on it. Or *into* it, for that matter. Of course, this being Sunnydale, all is not as it seems.

The Orb of Thesulah: A mystical sphere used in rituals of the undead. Or, alternatively, as a stylish new-age paperweight. You can, seemingly, buy one at your local magic shop ('Passion'). The Orb, however, is utterly useless without an accompanying ritual. Unfortunately, Jenny Calendar is brutally murdered by Angelus. Nevertheless, Angelus is not overly techno-savvy and believes that simply destroying the computer on which the ritual is stored will destroy the spell. (Obviously he's never heard of backing up on a floppy.)

The Gem of Amara ('The Harsh Light of Day'): The vampiric equivalent of the Holy Grail (although, with Spike on the case, it more resembles *Monty Python's Holy Grail*), The Gem of Amara is a stylish piece of jewellery, which renders the wearer invincible. Spike succeeds where previous generations of questing – if geographically limited – vampires have failed, and heads off into the sunlight. Where Buffy merely wrestles the ring from his finger and sends a smouldering Spike scurrying into the sewers. The ring is, subsequently, sent via Oz to Angel in Los Angeles. But that's another story.

The Word of Valios ('Doomed'): It's amazing what you can pick up at garage sales, especially if the garage belonged to a recently dead sorcerer. But Rupert Giles should, perhaps, have been a little more cautious about the inexpensive trinket that he acquired for his collection at one such event. He believed it was a cheap knock-off until a trio of demons intent on destroying the world arrived at his door. The Mark of Valios is, in fact, the last ingredient in The Sacrifice Of Three.

✍ The Box of Gavrox ('Choices'): The preparations for Mayor Wilkins's ascension are well under way. But the final piece of the jigsaw, The Box of Gavrox, comes to the attention of Buffy. In the ensuing hostage drama the box is opened, with fatal face-removing consequences for one hapless police officer ('Graduation Day', Parts 1 and 2).

✍ Anyanka's Amulet: When ninth-century Nordic housewife Aud takes imaginative vengeance on her unfaithful husband, Olaf, she comes to the attention of D'Hoffryn, Lord of Arashmaharr, he that turns the air to blood. He offers Aud immortality and gainful employment as a vengeance-demon ('Selfless').

- Aud becomes Anyanka, the patron saint of wronged women, and for 1,100 years she wields, mercilessly, the power of The Wish for the amusement of the Lower Beings.

- Her attempt to wreak vengeance on Xander Harris, on behalf of a scorned Cordelia, leads to the creation of a bizarre alternate reality. And, ultimately, to the capture and destruction of her power centre – her amulet – by Giles.

- Anya goes from being an all-powerful demon to a mortal teenager – and one who is flunking at math to boot ('Doppelgängland').

- A desperate attempt to enlist Willow's help to locate the amulet leads to more chaos and a suggestion that Anya should try looking for her amulet behind the sofa. In Hell.

✍ The Guardian's Axe ('End of Days'): Well, first, it's supposed to be a scythe, despite the fact that it looks nothing like

one. The weapon's shiny appearance belies the fact that it's been hidden for millennia. It is guarded, inevitably, by a guardian – the last of a collective of female proto-watchers who watched the Watchers (*Sed Quis Custodiet Ipsos Custodes?*). It's a pretty effective tool in the battle with The First. But it proves to be less essential to the outcome than Spike's soul-channelling sunshine device. Two *Deus Ex Machina*s for the price of one.

Outrageously sudden Californian Christmas Snow Storms ('Amends'): *Hallelujah*, it's a Christmas miracle. Angel is tormented by visions of his past wrongdoing, as The First, the ancient source of all evil, makes its inaugural appearance in Sunnydale.

- The ghosts of victims past appear to taunt Angel, and the late Jenny Calendar materialises to tell him that the only way to keep his soul is to kill Buffy.

- Tormented and guilt stricken, Angel decides to take his own life by waiting in the open for the dawn.

- Buffy eloquently attempts to dissuade him but, as dawn breaks, fate intervenes in the shape of magical Californian Christmas snow.

- As the lovers wander hand in hand through the streets of Sunnydale, with the snow up to their knees by this time, a sign on the Sun Cinema reads PRAY.

- Don't forget, children, this uplifting Christian message was brought to you by Joss Whedon, a self-proclaimed atheist. A definite case of a little less *Machina*, a little more *Deus*. As The King once said.

The Key: The biggest, most magical *Buffy* macguffin of all. The central mystery of Season 5. A plot-device so big it almost blocks out the sun.

- The Key is magical energy, created to open the doors between dimensions.

- Glorificus, a Hell-dimension goddess, is searching for The Key to help her escape from her bounds. (We'll ignore, for a while, the fact that her bounds include having to share her body with a young, male medical student. Because that way lies madness and sweaty palms.)

- The Key's guardians, a bunch of Central European monks, give it form, make it human and send it to Buffy Summers in Sunnydale to protect ('No Place Like Home').

- Thus, one recipe for *instant sister* ('Buffy vs. Dracula'). Dawn is, apparently, a typical teenager: brattishly annoying, perceptive, whiny and winning in equal measures ('Real Me').

- She's also, in reality, a ball of glowing green energy with the power to cause dimensions to collide … or something, because, frankly, the series is never entirely clear on this – some would say important – point.

- Dawn's disguise is near perfect but has one fatal flaw – mad people can see through the human construct into the emptiness beneath ('Listening to Fear') and have a habit of chanting either biblical nonsense or stuff related to nursery rhymes at the poor lass.

- When Glorificus is around, her brain-sucking the unlucky citizens of Sunnydale ensures that mad people are in plentiful supply ('Blood Ties').

167

- Accidentally betrayed by Tara ('Tough Love'), Dawn is captured by Glory ('Spiral') and prepared for a ritual sacrifice ('The Weight of the World').

- Glory needs a portal to get home, and she has no qualms about destroying this – or any other – world in the process ('The Gift').

- Dawn's blood falls and the dimensions begin to bleed into one another. Buffy, having already established that her own blood is the same as Dawn's, sacrifices herself and saves the world.

- Dawn becomes a real girl.

- Buffy dies. But in Sunnydale this isn't always a permanent state ('Bargaining' Part 1).

THICK AS THIEVES:
The complicated psyche, lives and loves of Spike, the second vampire with a soul – Part 8

✎ Spike is a loner and he rarely seems to have any real friends. Minions he's had plenty of, and he forms liaisons as a matter of business or in the pursuit of chaos ('Surprise', 'Innocence'). It's clear that Spike's only real relationships are with Drusilla and, later, Buffy. Harmony is convenient for sex but there's no sense of companionship. However, from the outset he likes Buffy's mother – perhaps because she reminds him of his own beloved mum. He also has a tender and protective relationship with Dawn. Yes, there is *definitely* something about those Summers women ...

✎ Getting captured and implanted with a behavioural chip leaves him vulnerable and with the options to starve or to form an uneasy alliance with the Scooby Gang ('Pangs'). It begins with a trade of information for food and protection, and with the Scoobies tolerating him (barely). When, trying to save his own skin, Spike discovers that he can hurt demons ('Doomed'), he finds a new purpose in life: fighting on the side of good for the sake of ... puppies and Christmas ... or something. If it seems, at times, that he really has joined the side of right, Spike is quick to reassure the Scoobies that this isn't the case, wondering if any of them can at least try to remember that he hates them ('This Year's Girl'). He is outraged when Dawn declares that she feels safe with him ('Crush').

169

✍ Spike's new lifestyle does not go down well within the Demon Community. Nobody likes a turncoat. His social life revolves around Willy's Alibi Bar, where he plays poker for kittens ('Life Serial') and fights off demons who call him on killing his own kind. However, he doesn't seem to be very good at winning any of these poker games he gets into, and finds himself in trouble with a loan shark ('Tabula Rasa'). There is, of course, the small matter of obtaining money for blood and smokes. So he develops a penchant for robbery with menaces ('Where the Wild Things Are').

✍ He helps Giles when the former Watcher becomes a Fyarl demon and, despite this being another cash transaction, the two seem to get along quite well. But Spike's reaction to Giles's suggestion that his acquisition of a chip may be, in some obscure way, a predestined event is outright ridicule. Giles is also, by far, the harshest member of the gang when Spike's true feelings towards Buffy are revealed. Angrily turning on Spike ('I Was Made to Love You'), Giles informs him that the Scoobies are neither his friends nor his way to Buffy.

✍ Giles retains his wariness of Spike, reluctantly accepting his help in fighting against evil and in taking care of Dawn after Buffy's death ('Bargaining' Part 1). But he is horrified when Buffy has Spike's malfunctioning chip removed ('First Date') and, ultimately, Giles becomes a co-conspirator in Robin Wood's plan to kill him ('Lies My Parents Told Me'). Surprisingly, he also shows a most un-Watcherly lack of interest after Spike gets his soul back. Granted, Giles has had some bad experiences with Angel ('Passions', 'Becoming' Part 2) but one might have expected at least some curiosity about Spike's new status.

✍ Xander and Spike have an equally rocky relationship. Xander is wary of the vampire. To be fair, he took much the same attitude with Angel – and for a similar reason, that there's a doomed obsession with Buffy at the core of them both. Spike did once knock Xander out, lock him in a burned-out building and threaten to kill him ('Lover's Walk'). The pair snipe at each other with alarming regularity and Xander's contempt when he discovers that Spike has slept with both Anya and Buffy is painful to watch. Yet, along the way the pair have shared moments of bonding, living as a very odd couple in, first, Xander's parents' basement ('Hush', 'Doomed') and, subsequently, Xander's new apartment.

Xander ties Spike to a chair to keep him from any temptation of midnight snacks, since Xander considers himself to be moist and deliciously biteable. Xander sympathises after Spike is beaten to a pulp by Glory ('Intervention'). According to Xander, Spike is compact, well muscled and kind of mysterious – it's little wonder that, while Buffy denies that *she* is sleeping with Spike, she suspects that Xander may be. This potential avenue reaches its climax in 'Beneath You' as Spike and Xander exchange worried glances when Nancy asks if there's anyone here who hasn't slept together.

The pair play pool and share a beer ('Triangle'), have a moment of understanding ('Spiral'), work out a cunning plan to rescue their women from the effects of a love spell ('Him') and, eventually, become housemates again ('Conversations With Dead People', 'Sleeper'). But it's Xander who discovers that Spike tried to rape Buffy and he, subsequently, made sure Dawn knew about it. Their relationship, thus, never progresses much beyond fear and contempt on Xander's side and a certain amused condescension on Spike's.

Willow and Spike have an even stranger relationship. While still the Big Bad, Spike kidnapped Willow and Xander

('Lover's Walk'). Spike certainly respects Willow's intellect but he also seems to find her not unattractive. In the aftermath of having been chipped by The Initiative, Spike tries to bite Willow and suffers from the vampire equivalent of impotence. The pair then comfort each other. Willow suggests that they try again later and wonders if it's because she's not attractive enough ('The Initiative').

It's Spike who notices how heartbroken Willow is when Oz leaves ('Wild At Heart'). It's also Spike, heartbroken himself by Buffy's rejection of him, who rejoices that Willow and Tara are back together ('Smashed'). And when Spike is in the biggest trouble of his life, Willow is the one who goes out to buy him pig's blood ('Never Leave Me'). While Spike professed not to care about the situation, it was he who helped to save Tara from her abusive family by simply, if painfully, proving that she was not a demon ('Family'). (The family myth about the women turning into demons when they turn twenty is just a bit of spin to keep the ladies under control. The fact that Spike seems to approve of this misogynistic plan doesn't lessen the helpfulness of his selfless deed.)

Spike knows a lot about the Scoobies. He is very perceptive and aware of the hopes, aspirations, fears and failings of others. It is, perhaps, this perceptiveness that enables him to work with Adam in an attempt to destroy the cohesion of the group, by using their own fears to set them against each other. It is, he notes, much like what happened to The Beatles after Yoko arrived – she didn't specifically split them up, she just happened to be there ('The Yoko Factor'). But, Spike's powers of perception appear not to extend to Adam duping him. So it's good that he keeps all of his options open and ends up helping in the fight against Adam and The Initiative ('Primeval').

Anya and Spike have a lot in common. Both have demonic pasts. Both are, for the most part, working on the side of good. Both know what it was like to have infinite power and then to have lost it. And both have problems in adjusting to the behaviours and social niceties demanded by human society ('Where the Wild Things Are'). Of all the Scoobies, Anya is probably Spike's favourite. In fact, he tells her, she's the only one of them that he can stand. He admires her because she's forthright and speaks her mind. When they have some brief, solace-based sex ('Entropy'), they separate with a mutual nod of respect.

It is Anya who first realises that Spike has a soul ('Beneath You'), and she is the only one who shows the degree of excitement and curiosity that this momentous feat deserves. Later, Anya is caught searching Spike's bedroom for evidence that he has reverted to his serial-killing ways but she seems not entirely adverse to the idea of them rekindling the flame of their brief encounter ('Sleeper'). When they go drinking together to avoid the horde of potential Slayers, Anya seems keen to see this as a date rather than just two friends having a beer. It seems somehow fitting that these comrades should both gain redemption through death in the final fight for Sunnydale ('Chosen').

Spike and Riley Finn *really* hate each other. Riley was part of the organisation that captured and chipped Spike and, worse, he shares Buffy's bed. Spike is jealous and resentful and it is he who breaks the couple up by revealing Riley's habit of visiting a vampire brothel ('Into the Woods') to Buffy. When a furious Riley arrives at Spike's crypt, intent on revenge, the two rivals fight then end up sharing a bottle of wine while discussing how much love, ultimately, sucks. When Riley returns to Sunnydale with his glamorous new commando wife ('As

You Were'), he destroys the crypt where Spike, having inexplicably become a demon-egg-dealing international criminal, is snuggled up to Buffy.

Spike takes a dig at Buffy's other boyfriends, including the despicable Parker Abrams ('The Harsh Light of Day'). He brings an extremely skanky Goth girl (possibly demon, though it's difficult to tell these days) to Xander and Anya's wedding ('Hell's Bells'). She seems, Buffy notes, like a nice attempt at making Buffy herself jealous – which works. But he sweetly leaves the ceremony when he realises just how much Buffy is hurting.

Spike has at least one proper friend – Clem, a loose-skinned demon who cheats at kitten poker ('Tabula Rasa'), loves snack food and becomes such a part of the gang that he also gets an invite to Xander's wedding. Clem hangs out with Spike, accompanies him to parties ('Older and Far Away') and forms quirky and rather touching friendships with both Dawn and Buffy ('Seeing Red'). It is Clem who tries to understand and comfort a distraught Spike after the disastrous encounter with Buffy that leads to his soul-quest. And it is Clem who looks after Spike's crypt in his absence. After helping with the training of the potential Slayers, Clem flees Sunnydale before the final fight. It is to be hoped that, in the aftermath of Sunnydale's destruction, Clem found a moment to mourn his friend's passing.

'IT'S A WHAT, NOW?':
25 words that we learned from *Buffy the Vampire Slayer*

You know a television show has made it into the popular consciousness when words that appear in it start cropping up in people's regular vocabulary. *Doctor Who* gave the world 'dalek' and 'TARDIS', *Star Trek* countered with 'energize' and 'phaser'. Many of these, eventually, find a place in the *Oxford English Dictionary* and, subsequently, immortality. Here are a few examples of *Buffy*'s lexicographical efforts:

'Hellmouth' ('Welcome to the Hellmouth') – n. The mouth of Hell situated beneath the library in the old Sunnydale High School, and beneath Principal Wood's office in the rebuilt version.

'Hottie' ('Welcome to the Hellmouth') – n. A very attractive member of the opposite sex.

'Sitch' ('Welcome to the Hellmouth') – n. The current state of affairs.

'Wiggins' ('Welcome to the Hellmouth') – n. Nervousness, the jitters or fright.

'Suckfest' ('The Harvest') – n. A collective pleasurable experience for vampires.

175

'Slayerettes' ('The Witch') – n. One who helps, supports or otherwise aids a Slayer in her Slaying-type tasks.

'Keyser-Soze'd' ('The Puppet Show') – vb. To mislead by deliberate misdirection or lies (from the character of Keyser Soze, the (possibly fictitious) villain in the movie *The Usual Suspects*).

'Slayage' ('Out of Mind, Out of Sight') – n. The total amount of Slaying done by a Slayer.

'Bitca' ('When She Was Bad') – n. A malicious, spiteful or sarcastic woman as observed by the lexicographically challenged (see also Harris, Xander).

'Übersuck' ('Inca Mummy Girl') – vb. The worst thing that has ever happened in the world. Ever. Bar none.

'Smoochies' ('Halloween') – vb. To snuggle up with one's honey in a comfortable position. Some overlapping of tongues may also be involved.

'Scoobies' ('What's My Line?') – n. A Slayerette with a significant grasp of popular culture, specifically the Hanna Barbera cartoon genre of the early 1970s.

'Therapyland' ('Ted') – n. A place inhabited by people who have just witnessed their mother French-kissing a man old enough to be their biological father. But who is, in fact, not.

'Freaksome' ('Phases') – adv. Causing fear or alarm.

'Cuddle-monkey' ('Bewitched, Bothered and Bewildered') – n. A young man who has extramarital sexual relationships with (usually, though not exclusively) older women.

'Foulness' (Go Fish) – n. A strong and offensive odour.

'Dump-o-gram' ('Revelations') – n. The sudden and unexpected realisation that one has just relocated to Dumpsville. Population: You.

'Guiltapalooza' ('The Wish') – n. Extreme remorse bordering on self-flagellation caused by the feeling that one is responsible for a perceived wrong.

'Clueage' ('Pangs') – n. Data upon which to base proof or establish a falsehood.

'Glowery' ('Pangs') – adv. To stare hard and broodingly, like a magnificent poof.

'Wanna-Blessed-Be' ('Hush') – n. & adj. An extremely silly girl, probably a university student, possibly lesbian, perhaps with a henna tattoo, who tries to emulate a Wicca lifestyle, and similar attitudes and *realpolitik* (specifically sexual *realpolitik*). But who seems desperately false and naïve to observers. Likely to misuse words like 'empowerment'. *Not* a sister of The Dark Ones.

'Revealy' ('The Replacement') – adj. To be revealed by revelation.

'Eeuch' ('Tabula Rasa') – n. A loud, if somewhat guttural, emotional cry of absolute terror.

177

'Patheticness' ('As You Were') – n. Ludicrously and distressingly inadequate or worthless.

 'Cartoony' ('Grave') – adj. Pertaining to a cartoon.

SLAYER

'I THINK I WAS IN HEAVEN':

12 great lines of dialogue from *Buffy*'s Season 6

Xander, to Willow: 'Who made you the boss of the group?' Anya: 'You did ... You said, "Let's vote," and it was unanimous ...' – 'Bargaining' Part 1

Giles, to Willow: 'The magics you channelled are more ferocious and primal than anything you can hope to understand, and you are lucky to be alive, you rank, arrogant amateur.' – 'Flooded'

Jonathan, to Andrew and Warren: 'Stop touching my magic bone.' – 'Life Serial'

Anya, on bunnies: 'They're not just cute like everybody supposes/They got them hoppy legs and twitchy little noses.' – 'Once More, With Feeling'

An amnesiac Spike: 'I must be a noble vampire. A good guy. On a mission of redemption. I help the hopeless. I'm a vampire with a soul.' An amnesiac Buffy: 'A vampire with a soul? How *lame* is that?' – 'Tabula Rasa'

Buffy: 'How've you been?' Amy: 'Rat. You?' Buffy: 'Dead.' – 'Smashed'

Buffy, on the drawbacks of her new occupation: 'That's just great. I try to do the simplest thing in the world, get an ordinary job in a well-lit place and, look, I'm back where I started. Blood and death and funky smells.' – 'Doublemeat Palace'

Xander, when Buffy tells him about the possibility that the entire last six years has been a series of her own feverish hallucinations: 'You think this isn't real just because of all the vampires and demons and ex-vengeance-demons and the sister that used to be a big ball of universe-destroying energy?' – 'Normal Again'

Tara, to Willow: 'Trust has to build again, on both sides ... It's a long and important process. Can we just skip it? Can you be kissing me now?' – 'Entropy'

Xander: 'I've had blood on my hands all day. Blood from people I love.' – 'Villains'

Willow: 'There's no one in the world with the power to stop me now.' Giles: 'I'd like to test that theory.' – 'Two To Go'

Xander saves the world: 'I loved crayon-breaky Willow and I love scary-veiny Willow. So if I'm going out, it's here. You wanna kill the world, you start with me. I've earned that.' – 'Grave'

'SUBTEXT RAPIDLY BECOMING THE TEXT':
25 films, television series, novels and other exterior sources that provided direct inspiration to, or were referenced in, *Buffy the Vampire Slayer*

Like many modern TV series (*24*, *Stargate SG-1*, *The Simpsons* and *The X-Files* are contemporary examples), *Buffy* appears to be the product of our increasingly interconnected multimedia age. In other words, it's a show produced by a bunch of thirtysomething fanboy (and fangirl) media-geeks who revel in knowingly sampling exterior texts into their work. They do this openly, in the belief that their audience are sussed enough to know what they're watching a homage to and, thus, to join in a celebration of that twilight *demi-monde* world between parody and tribute.

Intellectual parallelograms crop up all over the place in *Buffy*, in an outrageous mix of pop-culture allusions, acknowledged roots, visual references and aspects that may owe a more subtle debt to other texts. There has never, at any stage, been a suggestion of intentional plagiarism. Rather, *Buffy*'s writers have, whether consciously or unconsciously, defined their audience as a collective who have, more or less, the same DVD and comics collections that they themselves do.

Thus, in *Buffy*, we're treated to a never-ending stream of references: pop-culture, 'Generation X' and general homages to all things esoteric. This section contains a sampling:

181

🗡 In interviews, Joss Whedon has noted that two of his imme-diate conceptual inspirations for *Buffy* were a pair of stylistically fascinating late 1980s vampire movies, *Near Dark* (Kathryn Bigelow, 1987) and *The Lost Boys* (Joel Schumacher, 1987). Both caustically rejected many of the traditional motifs of the vampire genre (bats, capes and castles, not least amongst them) and also the absurd pretensions of Anne Rice's – then very popular – con-temporary vampire novels featuring the character of Lestat. Instead, both of these movies attempted to drag the vampire format kicking and screaming into the twentieth century.

🗡 That said, Hammer's 1966 classic *Dracula, Prince of Darkness* (Terence Fisher) provides a plethora of visual allu-sions in episodes as diverse as 'The Harvest', 'When She Was Bad' and 'Becoming' Part 1. Its sequel, *Dracula Has Risen From The Grave* (Freddie Francis, 1968), probably inspired the climactic finale to 'Prophecy Girl'.

🗡 *Buffy*'s regular use of non-linear flashbacks to provide information on Angel's back story (and, subsequently, that of Spike) appears conceptually inspired by Russell Mulcahy's 1986 cult movie *Highlander* and by the early-90s TV series *Forever Knight*, which concerned a vampire policeman seek-ing redemption of his centuries of sin.

🗡 *The X-Files*: One of the most iconic and savvy TV suc-cesses of the decade in which *Buffy* was created, the series and its central characters of Fox Mulder and Dana Scully are directly referenced in numerous episodes, including 'The Pack', 'Life Serial', 'Gone', 'Dead Things', 'Two To Go' and 'Lies My Parents Told Me'.

🗡 *Spider-Man*: The much-loved Marvel superhero is one of the most widely quoted texts in *Buffy*, with allusions to Peter

Parker and his secret crime-fighting identity cropping up in 'I, Robot ... You, Jane', 'Phases', 'A New Man', 'No Place Like Home', 'After Life', 'Flooded' and 'Two To Go'. In 'Crush', a porter at Sunnydale railway station is seen reading a copy of *The Amazing Spider-Man*.

Xander refers to 'With a little help from my friends' in 'I, Robot ... You, Jane', which seems a bit retro for him, frankly. Maybe his parents have a copy of *Sgt. Pepper's Lonely Hearts Club Band* lying around at home? Or, given Xander's subsequent misquoting of 'I Am The Walrus' in 'What's My Line?' Part 2, more likely a copy of *The Beatles 1967–70*. On a somewhat related note, the textbook that the invisible Marcie Ross is reading at the end of 'Out of Mind, Out of Sight' contains printed lyrics from the Beatles' 'Happiness is a Warm Gun'.

The notorious case of the Internet couple Robert Glass and Sharon Lopatka who fantasised about Glass killing Lopatka, to the point where Lopatka, allegedly, knowingly went to her death at Glass's hands, gained much publicity at the time of Glass's arrest in October 1996. It is probable that Buffy and Xander's hysterical speculative discussion about Willow's net-friend, Malcolm, in 'I, Robot ... You, Jane' is an oblique reference to this disturbing case.

Spike's outrageous bravado in front of the other vampires in 'School Hard' may be an oblique reference to the infamous 'Show us yer yarbles' sequence in *A Clockwork Orange* (Stanley Kubrick, 1972).

The name of Oz's band, Dingoes Ate My Baby, is a reference to the real-life case of Australian mother Lindy Chamberlain who was wrongly imprisoned for murdering her infant daughter, Azaria. The film dramatisation of these events was *A Cry in the Dark* (Fred Schepisi, 1988).

The characters of the ghosts James and Grace in 'I Only Have Eyes For You' share their names with those of the leading actors in Alfred Hitchcock's *Rear Window* (Stewart and Kelly, respectively).

Cordelia says that she has been doing 'the Vulcan Death-Grip' since she was four ('Homecoming'). Of course, all Trekkies know only too well that the Vulcan Death-Grip doesn't, in fact, exist. It was a ruse invented by Kirk and Spock to fool some gullible aliens.

Two *Buffy* episode titles share their name with songs written by English singer/songwriter Elvis Costello – 'Lover's Walk' and 'This Year's Girl'. There's also an allusion to Costello's song 'Big Sister's Clothes' in the dialogue of 'Graduation Day' Part 1.

Wesley's middle name – Wyndam – is a probable reference to the godfather of British science fiction, John Wyndham (1903–69), the author of *The Day of the Triffids*, *The Midwich Cuckoos*, *The Kraken Wakes* and *Random Quest*.

Buffy notes that when Billy Fordham ignored her in fifth grade she sat in her room for months listening to the Divinyls song 'I Touch Myself' ('Lie To Me'). She then adds, hurriedly, that she had absolutely no idea what the song was about. For anybody who *doesn't* know, it's a heartfelt celebration of masturbation.

Oz's guitar contains a sticker with the inscription SWEET J ('Bewitched, Bothered and Bewildered'), a probable reference to Lou Reed's classic Velvet Underground song 'Sweet Jane' (see also *The Harsh Light of Day*). However, this is also a really subtle *Austin Powers* in-joke, Sweet J being the name of Scott Evil's unseen best friend in *Austin Powers: International Man of Mystery*.

When asked by Riley if he has ever heard of The Slayer, Forrest replies, 'Thrash band. Anvil-heavy guitar rock with delusions of Black Sabbath' ('Doomed'). Riley himself seems to have slightly less questionable musical taste, quoting directly from the Sex Pistols' 'Anarchy in the UK' when threatened by Colonel McNamara ('The Yoko Factor').

Although based on a real-life Transylvannian warlord, Vlad Tepes (1431–76), Count Dracula as a character first appeared in Bram Stoker's eponymous 1897 classic. Several aspects of 'Buffy vs. Dracula' are drawn from this source – for example, the three sisters who menace Giles haunt Jonathan Harker in the book – and, also, from Tod Browning's legendary 1931 film adaptation. Xander's possession mirrors the character of Renfield, while Nick Brendon's performance in the episode owes much to that of Dwight Frye who played Renfield in the movie.

The Knights of Byzantium take their name from the ancient free city in Thrace, founded circa 660 BC by the Greeks. The Romans occupied Byzantium from AD 73, and it subsequently changed its name to Constantinople in AD 330. The city is now Istanbul, in Turkey. Byzantium of the Middle Ages was staunchly Christian and produced several crusades against the Muslims. Some viewers found the introduction of the Knights in 'Checkpoint' to be somewhat ridiculous, particularly Orlando's declaration, 'We are the Knights of Byzantium – an ancient order.' It must be said, however, that

185

the alternative, 'We are the Knights of Byzantium. We were formed last week down the pub for a laugh,' would have been a shade *more* ridiculous.

Possibly the widest range of references in a single *Buffy* episode occurs in 'Once More, With Feeling':

- The title is a quotation from Joan Armatrading's 'Love and Affection' (also alluded to in 'The Freshman').

- The trio of street-sweepers that Giles, Xander and Anya walk past appear to be performing the dance of the chimney-sweeps from *Mary Poppins*.

- Spike's 'Get your kumbayayas out' is an allusion to both the African hymn 'Kumbaya' and the Rolling Stones' 1970 live LP *Get Your Ya-Ya's Out*.

- Spike refers to '76 Trombones' from *The Music Man*.

- There are visual references to the title sequences of the James Bond movies (specifically *The Spy Who Loved Me*), Tim Burton's *Batman* (Sweet's 'Joker'-style suit and attitude), and Michael Powell and Emeric Pressburger's 1948 ballet masterpiece *The Red Shoes* (Dawn's dance with Sweet's minions).

- Also, *Pinnochio*, *Snow White and the Seven Dwarfs*, *The Karate Kid*, The Isley Brothers' 'Twist and Shout', *That's Entertainment*, *The Avengers*, *The Addams Family*, *Superman*, award-winning journalist David Brinkley, Peruvian mambo singer Yma Sumac and the stage musical *The Lord of the Dance*.

- Sweet claims to have bought the Emperor Nero (AD 37–68) his first fiddle (presumably the one that Nero, allegedly, played while Rome burned).

- Xander's 'Respect the cruller and tame the doughnut' paraphrases a very crude Tom Cruise line in the movie *Magnolia*, concerning male and female genitalia.

- 'Going Through the Motions' paraphrases Duke Ellington's 'It Don't Mean a Thing (if it Ain't Got that Swing)'.

✍ Unsure of his religious beliefs, an amnesiac Xander chants the traditional Christian prayer 'Now I lay me down to sleep', *Shema Yisrael*,[2] and the Buddhist meditation mantra 'Om' ('Tabula Rasa').

✍ The title of 'Older and Far Away' is a quotation from the novel *Empire of the Sun*. An issue of Neil Gaiman's award-winning comic *The Sandman* ('24 Hours'), concerning a group of people trapped in a diner, is conceptually very similar to this episode.

✍ When about to enter his trial by combat to regain his soul, Spike quotes Nirvana's 'Smells Like Teen Spirit' ('Two To Go'). The same episode includes possible allusions to *A Clockwork Orange*, *Christina F*, Neil Young's 'The Needle and the Damage Done' and Julian Cope's 1992 poem 'Hanging Out with Emma-Jane When Emma-Jane's a Junkie'. Another Spike allusion to a popular rock rebellion anthem

---

2 The beginning of one of the most important Jewish prayers: Shema Yisrael, Adoshem Elokainu, Adoshem Echud, which translates as: 'Hear, O Israel, the Lord is our God, the Lord is One', and appears in Deuteronomy 6:4.

occurs in 'Chosen' – in this case, Alice's Cooper's 'School's Out'.

In interviews, writer Jane Espenson has noted that Gnarl ('Same Time, Same Place') was, in part, based on the character of Gollum from *The Lord Of The Rings* trilogy. In realisation, however, the demon's voice is actually a dead-ringer for the leader of the Blue Meanies in *Yellow Submarine*. The character of Caleb ('Dirty Girls') was probably influenced by the misogynist preacher in Davis Grubb's *The Night of the Hunter*. (Robert Mitchum played the role in Charles Laughton's 1955 film adaptation.)

In 'The Killer In Me', Kennedy notes that she first discovered her true sexual orientation when she saw Vivienne Leigh's performance as Scarlett O'Hara in *Gone With the Wind* as a five-year-old. She says that she loves the way Willow always turns off the *Moulin Rouge* DVD at chapter 32 so that the movie has a happy ending.

Books glimpsed in Andrew's imaginary room when he's making his documentary ('Storyteller') include:

- *The Complete Works of William Shakespeare*

- Friedrich Nietzsche's *Beyond Good and Evil*

Somewhat inevitably, however, there are also vintage *Star Wars* posters on the walls.

SOMETIMES A CIGAR IS *JUST* A CIGAR:
Some examples of the use of metaphors in *Buffy the Vampire Slayer*

'I was a pathetic loser in school,' Joss Whedon once confessed and his stated intention was to make Buffy's conflict with monsters 'a metaphor about how frightening and horrible high school is'. Whedon has described how discussions in writers' meetings would involve questions like, 'What was the most embarrassing thing that ever happened to you in school?' and 'What is your favourite horror film?', followed by conversations on how these could be combined in an episode.

For some people memories of school are, as Muriel Spark describes them in *The Prime of Miss Jean Brodie*, the happiest days of their lives. For most of us, however, school was a time of intense pressure and crushing loneliness when, cruelly, we were nowhere near mature enough to deal with these emotions. That's the paradox of the teenage years that *Buffy* articulates so well. Many TV series have talked about how hard growing up can be. Few, however, have been as honest or as articulate about the process as *Buffy*. 'Basically, school is about alienation and horror,' Whedon has noted, although he's honest enough to admit, when asked, how like Xander Harris he himself was as a teenager: 'Less and less as he gets laid more and more.'

Whedon and the other writers, in using the clichés of horror movies – vampires, demons, possession, sci-fi robots – to represent the terrors of being a teenager and, subsequently, a young adult, have managed to tap into something buried deep within all of us. It's the subtext stuff – parental pressure, bullying, fear of sex, social exclusion. We empathise with the characters in *Buffy* because we were all once like them. Outsiders.

'Be careful what you wish for, it might come true': A key conceptual element in *Buffy*, used to varying degrees as character motivation – most obviously in 'Angel', 'Halloween', 'Bewitched, Bothered and Bewildered', 'Homecoming', 'Amends', 'Something Blue', 'Superstar', 'The Replacement', 'Tabula Rasa', 'Gone', 'Older and Far Away', 'Selfless' and 'Storyteller' – and absolutely central to 'The Wish' and 'Doppelgängland'. 'Be careful what you wish for' is one of those crass truisms that, on the surface, seem to state the obvious. Yet, as with most truisms, the underlying truth of the statement hides a deeper meaning:

- Xander's wish to be attractive to women.

- Cordelia's wish that Buffy had never come to Sunnydale.

- Buffy's wish to, literally, be someone else.

These desires become manifest in examples of wish-fulfilment that provide the desirer with more than they bargained for. Throughout *Buffy*, the theme keeps on cropping up (as late as 'Touched', the potential Slayers are given a caustic taste of 'be careful what you wish for' when they get a new leader but lose Buffy's experience as a fatal consequence).

'I slept with my boyfriend and he turned into a monster': A literal and bitter lesson of rejection that many girls experience during adolescence. This metaphor is central to 'Surprise' and 'Innocence', and the subsequent Angelus-arc covering the later episodes of Season 2. It is also seen – to a lesser degree – in 'Phases', 'Beauty and the Beasts', 'The Harsh Light of Day', 'Goodbye Iowa', 'Where the Wild Things Are', 'Wrecked' and 'All the Way' (and, if we take the metaphor to an extreme, in 'Hell's Bells' and 'Him').

- The cynical idea that all men are animals who are only interested in sex – articulated, angrily, by Faith in 'Beauty and the Beasts' – may have some truth in it, but it's a bleakly negative example of the series' view on growing up as a hard and lonely experience.

- Sex in *Buffy* is often a rather squalid and dangerous activity – a momentary release of repressed emotions, followed by guilt, aggression, suppression, confusion and pain.

'No one ever seems to notice me': The cornerstone of 'Out of Mind, Out of Sight', this metaphor is also used in a broader (and, occasionally, more positive) way in episodes as diverse as 'The Zeppo', 'Doppelgängland', 'Earshot', 'The Prom', 'The Freshman', 'Something Blue', 'The Yoko Factor', 'Real Me', 'Blood Ties', 'Gone', 'Normal Again', 'Help' and 'Storyteller'.

- In 'Out of Mind, Out of Sight', Cordelia appears sympathetic towards Marcie, the Invisible Girl, noting that it's awful to feel so lonely that you can, literally, disappear.

- When Buffy asks how *she* could possibly know this, Cordy asks if Buffy believes that Cordy herself is never lonely. She can be surrounded by people and still feel completely alone, she continues. After all, it's not as if any of

191

the people who want to hang out with Cordelia really know her.

- When Buffy asks why, if Cordy feels this way, she still works so hard at being popular, Cordelia says that it beats being alone all by yourself.

Which brings us to ...

The anger of the outsider: Just as *The Merchant of Venice* was a key reference text to 'Out of Mind, Out of Sight', so another Shakespeare play dealing with broadly similar subjects, *Othello*, is used as the template for 'Earshot'. As REM once said, 'Everybody Hurts':

- 'On the exterior [the series is] about demons and vampires and the mythology of the Slayer. But underneath it's strictly about growing up and all of that stuff just becomes a metaphor,' Kristine Sutherland has noted.

- Most *Buffy* episodes concern one form of outsider or another. Buffy herself, from the first episode, is a textbook example. A girl in a new town and school, struggling to keep her head above waves that could drown someone with less mental toughness (as it does with Marcie). Battling the preconceptions of others, whether it's hated authority figures like Snyder, or the expectations of her friends.

- Others deal with the pressure in different ways. Willow keeps her head down and hopes to avoid Cordelia's sarcasm.

- Xander becomes the class clown, with a witty comeback for every 'loser' put-down.

In 'Earshot', Buffy finds Jonathan alone on the top of the school clock tower with a gun in his hand.

- We've seen him in several episodes previously, a little fat kid who is, usually, the butt of cruel jokes by the likes of Harmony, or intimidated and bullied by others.

- Buffy tells Jonathan that she has never thought much about him and, she suspects, this is true of most of the students. This must really hurt Jonathan. He has all these feelings screaming inside of him and no one is paying any attention to him.

- Believe it or not, Buffy continues, she understands the pain.

- Jonathan is incredulous, echoing Buffy's own disbelief at Cordelia's similar confession in 'Out of Mind, Out of Sight'.

- Buffy replies that, on occasions, her life is more than she can handle. This is not just true of her, either, but of every single person. All of them are ignoring Jonathan's pain because they are too busy dealing with their *own*.

'This just can't get any more disturbing': In 'Doppelgängland', Willow experiences a literal presentation of the painful experience that many teenagers go through in discovering their true sexual orientation.

- Having summoned an other-dimensional vampire version of herself, Willow is horrified to discover that the creature is evil and skanky (and, as an aside, kind of gay – although evidence of her relationship with Xander in 'The Wish' suggests that Evil Willow is, actually, bisexual).

- Buffy reassures Willow, telling her that a vampire's personality has *nothing* to do with the person that it previously was.

- 'Well, actually ...' begins Angel. Then, thankfully, he shuts up.

- Subsequent revelations about the humans that Angel and Spike were – and, indeed, the sexual path that Willow herself takes – suggest that a vampire's personality has *much* to do with hidden aspects of the personality of the person it previously was.

'When we stop talking, we start to communicate': More than any other TV series in recent memory, *Buffy* took the concept of theoretical McLuhanism to its logical extreme. McLuhanism is the philosophy contained in the writings of Canadian media-guru Marshall McLuhan (1911–80), author of *The Medium is the Message*, which states that the *way* people communicate with each other is more important than *what* they actually communicate.

- This aspects is seen in numerous episodes, most especially in 'Hush'. 'Talking about communication, talking about language. Not the same thing,' notes Maggie Walsh in her lecture at the episode's beginning.

- In having Sunnydale's population lose their voices to demonic influence, 'Hush' makes the point that, often, talking gets in the way of true communication.

- Conceptually, 'Once More, With Feeling' takes this idea one stage further. In this, secrets and hidden agendas harboured by the members of the Scooby Gang are revealed

to both themselves and others, not through talking but
through song (and, again, only because a demon willed it
so).

- Other episodes that touch upon this complex narrative
  idea include 'I, Robot … You, Jane', 'Lie To Me',
  'Gingerbread', 'The Freshman', 'Restless', 'Crush', 'The
  Weight of the World', 'Gone' and 'Lies My Parents Told
  Me'.

How revealing is it that the name which Buffy chooses for
herself when she loses her memory – Joan – is that of a
legendary teenage warrior and, subsequently, martyred saint
('Tabula Rasa')? Messianic complex? Ooh, what a giveaway.

ZAP! BAM! POW!

Classic comic books, or characters from them, referenced or alluded to in *Buffy* include:

- The Human Torch from The Fantastic Four ('The Witch', 'Lessons')

- Batman ('Some Assembly Required', 'The Yoko Factor', 'Potential')

- Superman ('Reptile Boy', 'The Wish', 'The Zeppo')

- Power Girl ('Killed By Death')

- Judge Dredd ('Consequences', 'Selfless')

- The Avengers ('The Freshman', 'The Body')

- Captain Marvel ('Goodbye Iowa', 'Tabula Rasa')

- The Uncanny X-Men ('No Place Like Home', 'The Gift', 'Bargaining' Part 1)

- Captain America ('Shadow')

- The Incredible Hulk ('Tough Love')

- Nick Fury ('As You Were')

- Supergirl ('Normal Again')

LITTLE SISTER DON'T YOU DO WHAT YOUR BIG SISTER DONE:
The complicated psyche, lives and loves of Spike, the second vampire with a soul – Part 9

Dawn Summers is an unusual creature: she's a typical whiny – if highly intelligent and occasionally perceptive – teenage girl and also a mystical key, which unlocks dimensions. But, to Spike, she will always be Buffy's little sister and, as such, is to be protected up to and including the cost of his own life.

It is Spike's wish to protect Dawn that leads him to accompany her on a late-night raid to The Magic Box ('Blood Ties'), where he unwittingly reveals that she is not really Buffy's sister at all but, rather, a construct. Understandably this news upsets Dawn and she turns to Spike for comfort, hanging around in his crypt after school – albeit she horrifies Spike by telling him that she feels *safe* there ('Crush').

Dawn hangs out with Spike because he doesn't treat her like a child. She equates Spike with Angel. And Buffy loved Angel. When Buffy points out that Angel has a soul Dawn blithely replies that Spike has a chip – what's the difference? Later, trying to make sense of the tangled mess that is everyone's love life, Dawn returns to this recurring theme ('Him'). Why did Spike have to get a soul? How does that make him a better man? After all, a soul doesn't guarantee goodness – Xander had a soul when he left Anya at the altar.

197

Spike's protection of Dawn extends to him being beaten to a pulp by Glory rather than betray Dawn's secret ('Intervention'). It is in an attempt to protect Dawn that Spike is flung from the tower by The Doc ('The Gift') and the crushing burden of his failure to protect her fully leads Spike to him becoming, in effect, Dawn's minder, fighting with the Scoobies on the side of good and babysitting Dawn who, he is utterly determined, will never be hurt again ('Bargaining' Part 1). Spike even tries to persuade Dawn of the importance of school.

Once Buffy returns from the dead, Spike's role in protecting Dawn continues. It is Spike who takes care of her when Willow's misuse of magic leads to a broken arm ('Wrecked'). But Spike's relationship with Buffy causes Dawn problems. Spike seems more interested in shagging her sister than hanging out with Dawn like he used to ('Older and Far Away') and this, amongst other factors, leads to Dawn's growing problem of kleptomania. But it is still Spike to whom Dawn turns for protection, and, surprisingly, even after Spike attempts to rape Buffy ('Seeing Red'), the Slayer is willing to trust him enough to let Dawn take shelter with him ('Two To Go'). However, Spike has already left Sunnydale and she has to make do with Clem instead.

Dawn is in for a cruel disillusionment when Xander lets her know exactly what happened between Buffy and Spike. When Spike arrives back in Sunnydale, he is amazed to meet a furious and vengeful Dawn, an unbelievably scary creature who threatens to set fire to him in his sleep if he ever hurts her sister again ('Beneath You').

Buffy tells Dawn that Spike has changed and knows that he was wrong. It's no wonder that Dawn is confused. Buffy had declared that Spike disgusted her, yet she and he were at it like bunnies. Spike, who had *proved* his willingness to die for Buffy, ended up trying to rape her. Without trust, there can be no friendship, and sadly Spike and Dawn never resume their old, easy intimacy. Sometimes life is just too complicated, especially in Sunnydale.

SLAYER

'YOU MAY REMEMBER ME FROM SUCH FILMS AND TV SHOWS AS …':

15 further somewhat familiar guest stars on *Buffy*

Fans of *The X-Files* will recognise Brian Thompson (Luke in 'Welcome to the Hellmouth' and The Judge in 'Surprise') as the enigmatic Alien Pilot. He was also in *The Terminator* and *Star Trek: Generations* (playing a Klingon).

Mark Metcalf (The Master) played Doug Neidermeyer in the classic *National Lampoon's Animal House*.

Robin Riker (Catherine Madison in 'The Witch') was the female lead in the 1980 horror movie *Alligator*.

Aside from a brief stint in *Beverly Hills 90210* as Jill Fleming, Robia LaMorte (Jenny Calendar) was best known as Pearl in Prince's videos 'Diamonds and Pearl' and 'Cream'.

Armin Shimerman (Principal Snyder) played Pascal in *Beauty and the Beast* and then became a TV comedy icon as the Ferengi bar owner Quark in *Star Trek: Deep Space 9*. He also had a semi-regular role as a judge in *Ally McBeal*.

Dean Butler (Hank Summers in 'Nightmares') is best known as Almanzo in *Little House on the Prairie*.

Robin Atkin-Downes (the demon Machida in 'Reptile Boy') played the poetry-spouting telepath Byron in *Babylon 5*.

Robin Sachs (Ethan Rayne) appeared in Hammer's notoriously sexy *Vampire Circus* (1972). *Babylon 5* fans will recognise him as Hedronn. He also played the villainous Sarris in *Galaxy Quest*.

Vincent Schiavelli (Uncle Enyos in 'Surprise') has a CV that includes high-profile appearances in movies like *Ghost*, *One Flew Over the Cuckoo's Nest* and *Tomorrow Never Dies*.

Richard Herd (Dr Backer in 'Killed By Death') was James McCord in *All The President's Men*, Henry Skerridge in *Midnight in the Garden of Good and Evil* and Commander John in V. Readers may remember his performance as 'Captain Galaxy', Moe Stein, in *Quantum Leap*.

Jack McGee (Doug Perren in 'Becoming' Part 1) is one of those actors who seems to have been in *everything*. He appeared in *Backdraft*, *Lethal Weapon 2* and *Showgirls*, played a sheriff in *Basic Instinct* and was the cop who sprayed Val Kilmer with mace in *The Doors*.

Alexis Denisof (Wesley) can be seen in the video for George Harrison's 'Got My Mind Set On You'. He later played Richard Sharpe's love-rival, Johnny Rossendale, in *Sharpe* and appeared in *Rogue Trader*, *First Knight* (as Sir Gaheris) and the Vic Reeves/Bob Mortimer remake of *Randall and Hopkirk (Deceased)*.

Nick Chinlund (Major Ellis in 'Listening to Fear') may be familiar to readers as Billy Bedlam in *Con Air*.

201

Susan Ruttan (Doris Kroeger in 'Gone') had a cult following when she played Roxanne in *LA Law*.

Lee Garlington (Xander's mother in 'Hell's Bells') was Natalie's mom in *American Pie 2*.

SIGNS AND WONDERS:
What you can observe if you keep your eyes open in The Magic Box

Like most retail establishments, The Magic Box has its fair share of signs and notices.

- Some are informative (the price of scented candles, notices for forthcoming local events or bands playing at The Bronze).

- Others, prosaically, detail the rules of the establishment (NO SMOKING, NO CHECKS, PLEASE CHECK ALL BAGS/BACK-PACKS AT COUNTER).

- Most of these seem to have been inherited from the previous owners, including the late Mr Forgerty ('Real Me') who, like all of the shop's proprietors over the years, seem destined to live a shorter-than-average life.

- Some preserve the secrets behind the outwardly benign facade: for example, a large NO ADMITTANCE sign prevents curious customers from straying into Buffy's training room and trying out the gym facilities therein. (Although Xander and Anya *have* been known to indulge in some after-hours misuse of the equipment; especially the vaulting horse during 'Into the Woods'.)

- Given the shop's clientele, a DO NOT LEAN ON THE GLASS sign on the display cabinets close to the counter should, perhaps, also carry a warning about the inadvisability of mixing fragile vitreous surfaces with Troll Hammers ('Triangle'), very pissed-off Wiccans ('Two To Go', 'Grave') or flying vampires ('Lover's Walk').

- Certain promotional and advisory posters and banners are probably unique to Sunnydale: DON'T FORGET HANUKAH, CHRISTMAS, KWANZAA AND GURENTHOR'S ASCENDANCE ARE COMING! ('Listening to Fear') is a rather unusual, if laudably multicultural, seasonal invitation to part with your money.

- Devotees of Gurenthor who lack funds would be well advised to look elsewhere for their Mandrake root, chicken's feet, salamander eyes and Essence of Slug candles as SHOPLIFTERS WILL BE TRANSFIGURED ('No Place Like Home').

- The extraordinary profit margins and capitalistic pursuit of filthy lucre may also explain the lack of taste displayed in the, frankly, ill-advised HALLOWEEN BONE-ANZA promotion ('All the Way').

- Should any Sunnydale inhabitant share the view that the wares of the emporium are all just so much 'balderdash and chicanery', the resident thousand-year-old ex-vengeance-demon at the cash register can simply point them to the fact that MAGIC HAPPENS ('Family').

LOGIC, LET ME INTRODUCE YOU TO THIS WINDOW:
11 further things in *Buffy* that make absolutely no logical sense whatsoever

✊ The entire 'Angel's gypsy curse' subplot is *indescribably* dumb ('Angel', 'Surprise', 'Innocence', 'Becoming' Part 2). Angelus's punishment for killing one of the clan was to be given a soul. OK, *that* makes sense. But to take the soul away again if Angel ever gets happy, thus turning him *back* into Angelus, the vicious creature that killed thousands and, as a consequence, enabling him to kill even more ...? What the hell's *that* all about?

✊ The Flamingos' recording of 'I Only Have Eyes For You' is central to the episode of the same name and features in the numerous flashbacks to 1955. However, the song wasn't recorded and released until 1959.

✊ When they eat Ethan's demonic chocolate in 'Band Candy', why do all the affected adults, regardless of their actual age, speak and act as though their teenage years were during the 1970s?

✊ 'Doppelgängland' is based on a HUGE logic flaw. In 'The Wish', Anyanka used Cordelia's desires to create 'Dark Sunnydale', not as a parallel dimension but to *replace* normal Sunnydale. With the destruction of Anyanka's amulet by

205

Giles, version two of reality never existed. Put simply, either one Sunnydale can exist, or the other, but not both simultaneously. So, at the end of 'The Wish', Evil Willow and all the other 'Dark Sunnydale' characters never existed.

Who rings Buffy to tell her that Faith has woken from her coma in 'This Year's Girl?' It's certainly not Joyce – the very brisk nature of Buffy's replies suggest that she's talking to someone whom she doesn't know. The police would seem the obvious answer, but why would they ring Buffy with this information? Also, after a very brief call, Buffy knows huge amounts of detail concerning Faith's escape (that she knocked out someone and stole their clothes, for example). From the same episode, the nurse dials four numbers when she calls The Council of Watchers to inform them that Faith has escaped, which suggests an internal call – yet they subsequently arrive in a helicopter.

Glory specifically says in 'Blood Ties' that The Key could be anything from a bicycle pump to a log. Yet, when details of the ritual to restore The Key are revealed (in 'The Weight of the World'), it is blindingly obvious that The Key must be a human (in this particular case, Dawn) since blood is, as Glory notes, the key to The Key. Bicycle pumps or logs don't, generally, bleed.

Giles's flight from Sunnydale Airport in 'Bargaining' Part 1 is said to be 'leaving for Los Angeles and continuing to London'. US airports *do* sometimes use this description for flights that land at another US airport to take on more passengers. But the idea of a transatlantic flight originating in Sunnydale with a stopover in LA (just eighty miles away) is ludicrous.

- Given that, in most respects (specifically geographical), Sunnydale is based on the town of Santa Barbara, it is interesting to note that Santa Barbara Airport is a municipal (dealing chiefly with commuter flights to gateway cities like LA and San Francisco) and not an international one.

- Similarly, in 'Same Time, Same Place', Willow arrives on an international flight at Sunnydale Airport, yet she reaches the point where she expects to meet Buffy, Xander and Dawn carrying only hand luggage. That's not possible. Upon entering the US, baggage pick-up takes place *before* clearing immigration and customs.

How did Spike get all the way from Sunnydale to Africa ('Villains') in the timespan shown, and do so while avoiding any direct sunlight? Then, how did he get back to Sunnydale again? ('Lessons'). On a related note, Spike left his leather coat on Buffy's stairway banister before he attempted to rape her in 'Seeing Red'. When he subsequently left town, he was wearing a cloth jacket. The leather coat isn't seen again until Spike puts it on in 'Get It Done'. So when did Spike go back to the Summers' house to retrieve it and then store it away in the school basement?

Willow is referred to in several episodes as 'a Wicca' when the dialogue is clearly referring to her magical prowess, rather than to her as a practitioner of a group of pagan traditions of which witchcraft is only a small part. Not all Wiccas are witches and vice versa. It is ironic that a series that once so successfully lampooned trendy and inaccurate uses of Wiccan terminology by so-called 'Wanna Blessed-Bes' should be guilty of such crass errors themselves.

Worse, in 'Grave' we have a Wicca performing what is described as 'a satanic ritual'. That's a complete contradiction

207

in terms. Wiccas are pagans who don't believe in *any* Judaeo-Christian icons.

It is established that Sunnydale is a coastal town ('Go Fish'), with a dockyard ('Surprise', 'Consequences') and also at least one, and possibly two, sizeable lakes ('Once More, With Feeling', 'Help'). So, when the town disappears into a massive crater ('Chosen'), where does all the water go?

'THEY WANT AN APOCALYPSE? WE'LL GIVE 'EM ONE':
12 great lines of dialogue from *Buffy's* Season 7

Spike's description of his soul: 'I wanted to give you what you deserved. And I got it. They put the spark in me. Now all it does is *burn*.' – 'Beneath You'

Anya: 'Wouldn't it be tragic if you were being kind of silly with your comically paralysed sister while Willow was dying?' – 'Same Time, Same Place'

Olaf, trying to persuade Aud that he has no interest in Rannveig: 'Her hips are large and load-bearing. Like a Baltic woman … Your hips are small. Like a Baltic woman from a slightly more arid region.' – 'Selfless'

Xander, realising that Willow is affected by a love spell: 'RJ's a guy.' Willow: 'That's why I'm doing my spell. 'Cause, you know, he doesn't *have* to be.' – 'Him'

Warren, to Andrew: 'That was the *worst* attempted pig-slaughtering I've ever seen.' – 'Never Leave Me'

Xander, to Dawn: 'I see more than anybody realises, 'cause nobody's watching me … You're not special. You're *extraordinary*.' – 'Potential'

Anya, standing outside the bathroom: 'You've been in there for thirty minutes. What are you doing?' Andrew: 'Entertaining and educating.' Anya: 'Why can't you just masturbate like the rest of us?' – 'Storyteller'

Wood, to the vampire who murdered his mother: 'You took my childhood when you took her from me. She was my world.' Spike: 'And you weren't *hers*. Doesn't it piss you off?' – 'Lies My Parents Told Me'

Caleb, to The First: 'You're the fire that makes people kill and hate. The fire that will cure the world of weakness. They're just sinners. You *are* sin.' – 'Touched'

Buffy, on the solitude of command: 'I guess everyone's alone. But being a Slayer? There's a burden we can't share.' Faith: 'And no one else can feel it. Thank God we're hot chicks with super-powers!' – 'End of Days'

Angel, on Spike: 'Everybody's got a soul now. I started it, the whole "having a soul", before it was the cool new thing.' Buffy: 'Ohmigod, are you twelve?' – 'Chosen'

Buffy: 'I love you.' Spike: 'No, you don't. But thanks for saying it.' – 'Chosen'

DEATH OR GLORY:
7 season-ending cliffhangers that shaped the future of *Buffy*

The vampires are gone, The Master is dead and Buffy has closed the Hellmouth. As her friends gather in the library, Buffy notes that it has been a really weird day. Indeed, notes Xander, she died and everything. Giles says that he should have known that even death wouldn't stop her from getting the job done. Xander then reminds everyone that there is a dance at The Bronze tonight. It could be fun. 'We saved the world,' agrees Buffy. 'I say we party.' As they leave, Angel notes that he really likes Buffy's dress ('Prophecy Girl').

Buffy has sentenced Angel to Hell to save the world. However, in doing so, she has been forced to reveal her secret identity to her mother and been expelled from school. Joyce finds herself alone in Buffy's room. Some of her daughter's clothes are strewn on the bed. She sees a note amongst them. At Sunnydale High, Xander, Giles, Oz, Willow and Cordelia ask if anyone has heard from their friend. From a distance, Buffy watches them. Then she boards a bus. On the road, she passes a sign which reads NOW LEAVING SUNNYDALE: COME BACK SOON! ('Becoming' Part 2).

The Mayor's apocalyptic schemes have been defeated. Giles gives Buffy her diploma, which, he notes, he pulled from the flames of the burning school. Buffy feels someone watching

211

her. She sees Angel standing in the shadows. Then Angel slowly turns and disappears into the smoke and out of Buffy's life, perhaps forever. Buffy rejoins her friends and they discuss the fact that they survived high school. The final shot is of a half-burned Sunnydale High 1999 yearbook, with a cover that reads THE FUTURE IS OURS ('Graduation Day' Part 2).

Having survived strange and dangerous dreams, a side-effect of their summoning of the spirit of the first Slayer, the Scooby Gang wonder exactly what the Cheese Guy was all about. Buffy walks down the hall towards the bathroom. She turns and looks into an empty bedroom. She hears Tara's voice telling her, 'You think you know what's to come, what you are. You haven't even begun' ('Restless').

Buffy drives from the tower into the portal opened by the spilling of Dawn's blood. She has just told Dawn that she loves her but that this is something she has to do. Dawn has to be strong, she continues. The hardest thing in this world is to live in it. Next, we see a gravestone. It's sunny and a small bunch of flowers lies on the grass in front of it ('The Gift').

BUFFY ANNE SUMMERS

1981–2001

BELOVED SISTER

DEVOTED FRIEND

SHE SAVED THE WORLD

A LOT

Xander's bravery has saved the world from the wrath of Dark Willow's pain for revenge. The pair lie in each other's arms, weeping. Buffy tells Dawn that she is proud of her and that there is much she wants to show her as the pair crawl out of the grave and into the daylight. Meanwhile, in an African cave, Spike lies beaten and bloody. A demon tells the vampire that he has endured the required trials. He returns to Spike that which he most desires. His soul ('Grave').

Sunnydale is a crater in the desert. Buffy, Dawn, Giles, Xander, Willow and Faith look astonished at the devastation they have left behind them. Faith notes that it looks as though the Hellmouth is officially closed for business, though Giles reminds them that there is, in fact, another one in Cleveland. We saved the world, notes Xander. Willow adds that they *changed* the world. She can feel that, all over, there are Slayers awakening everywhere. They will find them. Faith ask Buffy how it feels to no longer be the sole Slayer and Dawn wonders what they are going to do now. Buffy looks back at the crater and smiles ('Chosen').

A LOVE LIKE BLOOD:
The complicated psyche, lives and loves of Spike, the second vampire with a soul – Part 10

⚡ From the moment that Spike first sees Buffy, it is evident that his fascination with her goes well beyond a simple interest in killing Slayers. He watches her dancing at The Bronze, stalking around on the periphery of the crowd like a prowling big cat observing his prey ('School Hard').

⚡ Having failed to kill her on his first attempt, he studies video footage of her technique ('Halloween'), remarking that this baby likes to *play*. When Angelus threatens his relationship with Drusilla and Spike enters into a bizarre alliance with Buffy to stop the rise of Acathla, his opening words to her are 'Hello, cutie' ('Becoming' Part 2) – no wonder Drusilla accuses him of having his head full of the Slayer ('Fool for Love').

⚡ Once back in Sunnydale, Spike takes time out from his latest attempt to slay the Slayer to taunt Buffy about her sexual life, something that he seems to take a particular interest in. He also has a great respect for her abilities in battle. When captured by The Initiative, Spike's first thought is that Buffy is, somehow, to blame.

⚡ Buffy, too, seems to have mixed feelings about Spike from the start. She certainly has a singular lack of success in killing him – allowing him to escape time and time again. She also notes that she can't fool Spike: he's the one person, other than herself, who always knows the truth about her ('Lover's Walk'). Buffy seems to be aware of Spike's physical reaction to her, once taunting the chipped and chained-up vampire with a – frankly sexual – invitation to bite her tender and throbbing neck.

It somehow seems quite natural that the two should react so well to Willow's spell-casting and end up engaged. Note that the spell said nothing about them loving or even liking each other, merely that they should get married. Yet there they are, canoodling away like the world's happiest and most disgustingly lovey-dovey couple ('Something Blue').

Over the next couple of years, Spike works reluctantly with the Slayer and it is evident that his obsession with her has not gone unnoticed by others. When Faith achieves a bodyswap with Buffy ('Who Are You?'), she taunts Spike with disturbingly alluring images of what she could do to him. Seemingly with the result that he will pop like warm champagne. Spike is intrigued, aroused and furious all at the same time, promising revenge if ever he should get that accursed chip out of his head.

This incident marks a turning point in Spike's relationship with Buffy and his obsession with her begins to mutate into stalking. He uses a mannequin in a blonde wig to work off his pent-up aggression ('The Replacement'); dreams about her ('Out of my Mind'); fantasises about her during sex with Harmony ('Family'); and lurks outside her house, unhappily observing her interactions with Riley ('No Place Like Home').

When Buffy and he talk about Spike's conquest of past Slayers, the mood becomes charged and erotic. The couple fight, then Spike leans in for a kiss. 'C'mon, Slayer,' he pants, 'you *know* you wanna dance.' Buffy's rejection of him is total and brutal – but not enough to dampen Spike's ardour apparently, as he sets out to kill her but ends up, instead, comforting her ('Fool for Love').

Matters reach a climax, so to speak, when Spike kidnaps Buffy after, horrified that Spike has a crush on her, she has given him the brush-off. Instead, she is chained up. (Note to Spike: When attempting to prove your love for a lady, the use of a cattle prod is not generally recommended.) Despite the utter (and predictable) failure of his plan, Spike still seems to hope that Buffy will eventually fall for him.

He continues his stalking and follows Riley to a vampire brothel. He then, helpfully, takes Buffy to see Riley's betrayal for herself. And yet, when a furious Riley arrives at his crypt intent upon revenge, Spike tells him that he envies Riley so much it chokes him because Spike himself knows that he has no chance with Buffy. He also seems very worried about Buffy's well-being after her break-up with Riley ('Triangle').

Perhaps the creepiest aspect of Spike's Slayer-obsession is his commissioning of a Buffy android replica from Warren Meers. It's *exactly* like Buffy in every detail. Only much nicer. Programmed, in a variety of ways, to make Spike happy. Ironically, it's this sex toy that leads to him being captured and tortured by Glory. His refusal to betray Dawn, despite sickening torture, leads to his sweetest reward. A kiss of honest gratitude from the real Buffy ('Intervention').

From this point onwards, the two begin to fight alongside each other. In a final gesture of reconciliation, Buffy invites Spike into her house before the final battle with Glory ('The

Gift'). Spike is overwhelmed. 'I know you never loved me,' he tells her. 'I know that I'm a monster. But you treat me like a man.'

Even after Buffy's death, Spike doesn't forget his love for her or his promise to protect Dawn. He stays in Sunnydale fighting evil and acting as a babysitter, unaware of Willow's resurrection plans. When a bewildered Buffy returns from the grave, it is Spike who tenderly cares for her. He has, literally, counted the days since her death and every night, in his dreams, he relives that final fight. Only, on these occasions, he is stronger, faster, cleverer and always he saves her.

The pair become attracted to each other, perhaps through mutual loneliness. Spike is the only person to whom Buffy can admit her true feelings. But, on some level, she still holds the soulless Spike in contempt. The two kiss ('Once More, With Feeling'), then kiss again ('Tabula Rasa'). But Buffy cruelly dismisses these incidents as loathsome and irrelevant and, when Spike realises that his chip doesn't function on her any more and that returning from the dead has made Buffy somewhat less than human, the pair fight ('Smashed').

In the middle of a raging battle, Buffy pushes Spike against a wall, kisses him again and then initiates a violent sexual encounter that, literally, brings the house down ('Wrecked'). This sets the pattern for a confused and abusive relationship, which subsequently develops. In this, time and again, Buffy initiates angry, violent sex and then, afterwards, rejects Spike while he, in his turn, seems to exercise control over her, leading her to explore options that both excite and, simultaneously, disgust her.

Spike wants to bring Buffy into the dark with him; Buffy is desperate for her friends not to find out about their relationship.

217

Tara is the only one to whom she can pour out her guilt and self-loathing. Why does she let him do these things to her? Moreover, why is it so often she who initiates encounters and can't stay away? It is the classic 'hurt/comfort' state in which two vulnerable and emotionally immature people become involved with each other in a way that satisfies a deep psychological need, if not, necessarily, any actual desire.

Buffy's self-abasement spills over into a savage beating of Spike in an alley ('Dead Things'). Believing that she's killed an innocent girl, Buffy suffers a terrifying, erotic nightmare full of lesbian overtones, penis and bondage metaphors (stakes, handcuffs), and guilt with a capital G.

Subtext: Buffy is so appalled by her continued involvement in an abusive tryst with a vampire unredeemed by a soul, and by her shame that, after two essentially noble boyfriends, she has been reduced to *this*, she is seeking some severe punishment for it. As her mom is dead and a spanking's probably out of the question, what better than a long stretch in prison? Dawn is correct when she says that Buffy's unhappiness since she came back from Heaven is partly the reason that she is so keen to go to the police. Jail, in many respects, is an ideal place for people who don't want to deal with their more complex issues. Buffy *has* responsibilities – both as a surrogate mother to Dawn and as the Slayer to the world at large – neither of which she can walk away from no matter how tempting that solution may be.

Finally, when Riley returns to town with his new and perfect life and his new and perfect wife, Buffy tells Spike that it's over between them. She has just been using him, she says, and though Spike might not be complaining the knowledge of what she had been reduced to is killing her. Buffy tells Spike to move on, but is horrified when his moving on includes some mutual solace with Anya ('Entropy').

Buffy is even more hurt when she has to face Xander's disgust at the revelation of her own sexual history with Spike. Meanwhile, Spike's self-esteem and self-respect are repeatedly crushed underfoot. His relationship with Buffy had always been based on violence – fighting and fornication. Maybe it's not surprising, therefore, that when Spike visits Buffy to try and rekindle their affair he badly misreads all the signs.

What begins as a discussion about 'where do we go from here?' ends in a violent – and completely unforgivable – sexual assault. Following which, with Buffy's words of rejection and disgust still ringing in his ears, Spike heads out of Sunnydale and embarks on a quest to regain the one thing that Buffy has constantly told him he lacks. The man who was so often mocked as a disgusting soulless thing goes out and, with bravery above and beyond the call of duty, earns himself a soul.

When the souled (and insane) Spike returns to Sunnydale, it is to a Buffy who flinches from his touch but who gradually comes to see that her abuse of Spike was, at least partially, responsible for what happened. As Buffy tells him, 'You fought the monster inside of you and you won. I believe in you' ('Sleeper'). It is this belief that sustains Spike through the torture inflicted on him by The First and its various minions.

Buffy, having rescued Spike ('Showtime'), spends time supporting his recovery, defending his place within the team as their strongest warrior and using him to help her train the potential Slayers ('Potential'). She also calls in a favour from Riley and, when The Initiative chip begins to malfunction, she

219

has it removed ('The Killer In Me'). She trusts Spike to stay on the side of right. He has, after all, a soul now.

When Giles and Robin Wood conspire to kill Spike because of his potential threat to the group, she coldly rejects them ('Lies My Parents Told Me'). Yet the couple do not rekindle their physical relationship until, at the lowest ebb of her life, turned out from her own home by her sister, it is Spike who finds Buffy and comforts her, loving her for – simply – who she is. The couple are content to lay in each other's arms and, as Spike watches her sleep, it is, he will subsequently note, the happiest night of his life ('Touched').

Being Spike, of course, he's utterly terrified of this new intimacy. By the time the final fight comes to Sunnydale, Buffy has admitted to Angel that Spike is in her heart ('Chosen'). As the last battle reaches its climax and Spike begins to burn, Buffy finally tells him that she loves him. Their linked hands smoulder as Spike replies that, no, she actually doesn't. But he thanks her, genuinely, for saying that she does. Spike's love for Buffy not only gave him his soul back, it also literally saved the world.

DID YOU KNOW ...?:

20 bits of completely useless trivia that utterly
defy categorisation from *Buffy the
Vampire Slayer*

In 'Who Are You?', Faith uses a credit card that she finds
in Joyce's house to ring the airport and book a ticket out of
Sunnydale. It most probably belongs to Joyce but it could,
just, be Buffy's. The expiry date, she notes, is 05/01 (May
2001). Can it be a coincidence that this was the exact month
– just over a year later – in which Buffy did, indeed, expire
('The Gift')?

Mutant Enemy, Joss Whedon's production company and
the makers of *Buffy*, *Angel* and *Firefly*, takes its name from a
line in the song 'And You, And I' by prog-rock dinosaurs Yes.

Sarah Michelle Gellar has a phobia about cemeteries. As
she told *FHM* in 1999, 'I used to cry if I went near one ... The
first series was a horrible nightmare, so for the second they
had to build fake cemeteries.'

'Bewitched, Bothered and Bewildered' is producer Gareth
Davies's favourite episode, but for very unusual reasons. As he
told *Entertainment Weekly*, with Gellar off the set for five
days hosting *Saturday Night Live*, the writers had the idea of
turning Buffy into a rat. 'Nothing against Sarah, but that rat
was *marvellous*. It was a real trouper!'

In Mike Hodges's 1987 film *A Prayer For The Dying*, Tony Head plays a cockney thug named Rupert. For his legion of female fans, it's a movie well worth checking out as he removes most of his kit during the course of it.

The list of Stevenson Hall residents, which Spike looks at in 'The Initiative', includes *Buffy* production staff members Jeff Pruitt (Stunt Co-ordinator), David Solomon (Co-Producer) and Lisa Rosenberg (Hair Stylist).

Asked by *E! Online* about her relationship with former *Buffy* co-star Alexis Denisof, Alyson Hannigan noted, 'I had a crush on him the moment he showed up on set. He was the good one who said, "Not while we're working together." We became friends, and I was dating somebody else [Marilyn Manson drummer Ginger Fish]. When that didn't work out, he was on *Angel* and we started dating.'

As reported in several UK newspapers in early 2001, four-teen-year-old schoolgirl Heidi Rogan, from Middlesbrough, bravely fought off an attack by five teenage male thugs, using martial arts moves she learned from watching *Buffy*. Finding herself surrounded, Heidi pole-axed one assailant with a punch. She followed this with a jump-kick to the groin of another. The other three cowards promptly fled. 'Buffy is my hero and I think she would have been proud,' Heidi was quoted as saying.

Sarah Michelle Gellar once used an interview with *Cosmopolitan* to pay tribute to her mother: 'Everything I am is because of my mom.' She was much less effusive about her father, who divorced her mother when Gellar was seven, describing him as non-existent in her life. Pressed to elaborate, she borrowed Keanu Reeves's line from *Parenthood*: 'You need a licence to go fishing, you need a licence to drive, but any butt-reaming asshole can be a father.'

The robot-girl, April, in 'I Was Made to Love You' was written specifically with teen-pop sensation Britney Spears in mind. Various scheduling clashes ultimately nixed any chance of Spears appearing.

Sarah Michelle Gellar intended to have someone else sing her songs in the musical episode 'Once More, With Feeling', which she would then lip-synch to. However, when she realised how emotional they were, she didn't want anyone else singing them. Alyson Hannigan, on the other hand, was so unconfident concerning her voice that she specifically requested to have no song of her own and very few singing lines in the ensemble pieces.

You always know when a TV show has reached the merchandise hall of fame when you can buy a pair of knickers with its name on them. Such an honour was bestowed on *Buffy* in 2002. The black pants, emblazoned with a Slayer logo, are currently only available in small or medium sizes. Large and extra large versions are, apparently, on the way.

The exterior location used for the Doublemeat Palace diner is a famous hot-dog restaurant called Hipperty Hopperty Dog, which can be found on Sepulveda Boulevard close to Los Angeles airport. 'Doublemeat Palace' is, incidentally, the only *Buffy* episode that ever caused advertisers to pull out their support from the series.

Anyone jittery about American competence in the war against terror may be relieved to learn about Anthony Cordesman, a professor at the Center for Strategic and

International Studies, an influential Washington think-tank that helps formulate US defence policy. In 2002 he wrote a treatise entitled *Biological Warfare and the Buffy Paradigm*. 'I would like you to think about the biological threat in terms of *Buffy the Vampire Slayer*; that you think about the world of biological weapons in terms of the "Buffy Paradigm"; and that you think about many of the problems in the proposed solutions as part of the "Buffy Syndrome".' For any three-star generals who were bemused by this, Cordesman prefaced his work with a word of explanation: *Buffy* is, he noted, 'about a teenage vampire slayer who lives in a world of unpredictable threats where each series of crises only becomes predictable when it is over'. Aren't you *beyond* glad that you live in a world where Buffy helps the President to decide who to bomb next?

Filming for the scenes in 'Lessons' and 'Beneath You' featuring Giles and Willow took place at Tony Head's home in the village of Timsbury, near Keynsham. Tony told the *Bristol Evening Post* that 'Joss suggested we use my place and I thought it might be fun. My only regret is the weather.' Afterwards, Whedon is reported to have motored to London and spent three hours buying comics in Forbidden Planet. Now *there's* a man who's got his priorities in life sorted.

The original script for 'Sleepers' featured a different song used to trigger Spike into his killing spree – 'I'll Be Seeing You' rather than 'Early One Morning'.

'I think the method is conducive for film and television because the method [involves] suspending your disbelief like you're asking the audience to,' James Marsters noted during a 2002 convention panel. 'You build an imaginary world and then release yourself into it. As sick as it sounds, in my head

224

there is a little Sunnydale, and a Buffy and a Spike. And Spike *loves* Buffy.' In more recent interviews, however, Marsters has noted that using method acting for TV is not a good idea as the actor has to sustain a character for too long. If, as in Spike's case, the character is being tortured or abused, this can really mess with the actor's head. Nevertheless, his *Buffy* colleagues apparently find James's working methods amusing. 'Sarah is *always* making fun of me,' James told the DragonCon audience in 2003. '"Oh, I'm a tree."'

After Willow enters the science lab and stands next to the dead hatchling in 'Bad Eggs', on the blackboard behind her is written POSTING BOARD. This was an acknowledgement (by Jeff Pruitt) to all the regulars on the *Buffy* Posting Board, *The Bronze*. In the same episode, when Joyce enters the library, keep your eyes on the standing sign. Under SUNNYDALE HS LIBRARY it says: WEBSITE COMING and BVS BRATS TALK, further acknowledgements of the series' many Internet fans.

Willow's line about the 'chocolatey goodness' of Oreo cookies in 'Go Fish' may be an in-joke, Alyson Hannigan having done several commercials for Oreos.

Just as *Buffy* was ending (indeed, a matter of days after the production's wrap party had taken place in a huge blaze of publicity at the Miauhaus studio), the British tabloid newspaper the *Daily Star* continued its impressive reputation for totally accurate reporting. They noted that ex-*Neighbours* actress and sometime pop wannabe Holly Valance was 'in discussions to replace Sarah Michelle Gellar in *Buffy*'. Yes, *of course* she was. Meanwhile, back in the real world ...[3]

[3] As a footnote, it's worth reporting Joss Whedon's first question when told of this 'exclusive' by the BBCi website. 'Who's Holly Valance?'

WHERE DO WE GO FROM HERE?:
Likely destinations for the Scooby Gang after the destruction of Sunnydale

From stray information given in four *Angel* episodes – 'Just Rewards', 'Harm's Way', 'Damage' and 'The Girl in Question' – we know (or can speculate) the following about what happened to these characters, whom we've got to know so well.

🗡 Buffy: In Europe, according to Angel. Indeed, it's easy to imagine Buffy chilling out in Rome or on some beach in the South of France once the burden of being the sole Chosen One was lifted. One thing is certain, however – she is unlikely to remain inactive for very long.

🗡 Dawn: It seems that Buffy has packed Dawnie off to a Catholic boarding school in Italy to finish her education.

🗡 Giles: Rebuilding the Council of Watchers somewhere in the Cotswolds. Seemingly with the help of 'several key Sunnydale *alumni*' whose number include Andrew (and, probably, Robin Wood).

🗡 Xander: In Africa, searching for Slayers. And, perhaps fruitlessly, for true love. Ah, bless …

🗡 Willow: Having some Wicca-related lesbian fun with Kennedy in Brazil (they're supposed to be based in Sao Paolo, but every time Andrew rings them they're in Rio).